SHOPLIFTING

SHOP-LIFTING

by L.B. Taylor, Jr.

Franklin Watts
New York | London | Toronto | 1979

Library of Congress Cataloging in Publication Data

Taylor, L   B
   Shoplifting.

   Bibliography: p.
   Includes index.
   SUMMARY: Discusses the possible causes,
popular preventative measures, and legal
implications of one of the fastest-growing
crimes throughout the world.
   1.   Shoplifting—Juvenile literature.
2.   Shoplifting—Prevention—Juvenile
literature.   [1.   Shoplifting]
I.   Title.
HV6652.T38   364.1'62   79–10076
ISBN 0–531–02877–1

CONTENTS

CONTENTS

FOREWORD

This is a book about young people and one of their problems. It is also an account of an important social change —a transformation of attitude and opinion on the part of young and old alike. There are a good many harsh realities discussed here as well as some thoughtful suggestions toward the solution of these difficult problems. Ultimately the book outlines a great deal of unfinished business, on everyone's part.

The last decade has been almost revolutionary in character with respect to relations between the generations. The tensions generated during the late 1960s led to some major redefinitions of what youth owed to age, and age to youth. The draft disappeared, mixed dormitories became a fact of life on college campuses, teen-age abortions could often be obtained without parental consent, and even marijuana smoking moved toward decriminalization. In short, standards shifted; youngsters demanded and got far more privileges than were once considered their due, and they took a number of liberties that were, in fact, never agreed to by the adults in their environment, but which everyone (parents, police, schools) seemed helpless to prevent.

Among these shifts was a rise in teen-age shoplifting, and a radical change in the mores that governed this behavior. There appeared a widely held attitude that it was acceptable, possibly even virtuous, and certainly great fun to rip off the establishment. Some of this was perhaps part of the new opulence, but much of it clearly had to do with the more general transformation of values. Many youngsters felt that it simply wasn't all that wrong; you probably wouldn't be punished if caught, or at the worst, you might have to make the purchase (just as if you broke something). In a way, it wasn't real; it was just play.

Shoplifting can have a lot of meanings. It can mean getting even, getting back at someone who treated you badly. (It's not exactly the same someone, but that part you sort of imagine. . . .). It can mean turning the tables instead of being the victim all the time; for once one is the predator, while the other fellow gets taken. It can mean outwitting, living out a daydream of being brave, skillful, and daring, and pitting one's ingenuity against the frowning presence of the Powers That Be, and tweaking their nose. It can give a feeling of wholeness, as though some part of the self were missing (maybe stolen away?) and is now recovered. It can allow for the impression of rage; you're angry so you rip someone off and you feel better. It can serve as a kind of put down; someone thought they could lord it over you but you showed them, and you're one up on them. It can have a group meaning, that is, to prove to others that you're not scared, you're not chicken, you'll do anything anyone else can do. It can give one a sense of excitement and fun, like going on a roller coaster or a ferris wheel; there is the special pleasure of doing something scary and overcoming the fear. One has proven oneself. It can even serve as a means of challenge: "OK, I'm taking what's yours, so what are you gonna do about it?" Or it can simply be the result of a lot of explaining to the self. "I need it, I have so little, and they'll never miss it . . . they have so much!" This is the rationalizing that allows a person to do just about anything they feel like doing. But perhaps most common of all is the feeling that shoplifting is all a form of play. One is engaged in a game; it's not really serious.

It takes no great amount of observation to perceive that one factor in the recent "set" of many an American youth is this sense of child's play. It is as though certain behaviors have become defined for these young people as larks, adventures, sporting events. One can smoke dope and, even if caught, nothing much will happen. One can have intercourse and no parent with a shotgun is waiting in the wings. One can shoplift and, if caught, it's like losing points in a game; it's unfortunate but minor, reversible.

Perhaps no trait so distinguishes youth from maturity as the notion of the irreversible. A grownup knows that whatever you do, you do; it can't be undone, and like it or not, you live with the consequences. This is one of the definitions of responsibility, and one of the bitterest lessons that comes with growing up. Children never believe it. For them, things will always somehow be set right, there will always be a grownup along to pick up the pieces. Even if death or divorce occurs, for years after a child may cling to the fantasy of reencounter with the lost one, or reunion of those who are parted. (Nor is the child within every grown man and woman so much different; the cost at which its pleadings and beckonings and reckonings must sometimes be put aside, and reality confronted in all its grimness is well within this ambience.) Armed with a spirit compounded of grandiosity, animosity, and playfulness (in varying proportions), the teen-ager couches lance to tilt with the storekeeper. There's a shop full of goodies waiting there to be had for the taking. And with a spirit of jocularity, defiance, or one-upsmanship, the taking proceeds—to the tune of millions of dollars a year the country over.

DR. JOSEPH NOSPHITZ
Director of Education and Training
Department of Psychiatry
Children's Hospital
National Medical Center
Washington, D.C.

SHOPLIFTING

INTRODUCTION

In the past few years, shoplifting has become one of the fastest-growing crimes in the United States and Canada, and, indeed, all over the world.

In America alone, four million shoplifters are caught in the act each year. Yet this is but the tip of a disturbing criminal iceberg. According to data from authoritative studies, there are an estimated 140 million instances of shoplifting in the United States each year, which means that for every thief apprehended, thirty-four get away.

This national epidemic of stealing adds up to a staggering $2 million in lost merchandise annually.

Studies also point out that half of all shoplifters today are teen-agers.

Who are these young thieves, and why do they steal? It is a complex question, not easily answered. Experts do know, however, that girls are most likely to shoplift between the ages of fifteen and seventeen, and boys from twelve to fifteen, although the age range is by no means confined to these particular age groups. Statistics show that many children begin stealing in stores at about age ten.

Surprisingly, only a small percentage of teen-agers steal out of need. Most of those caught come from solid middle-class families, and had enough money on them to pay for the items they took.

Teen-agers apparently steal mostly for the following reasons: for kicks; because "everyone" does it; because the store "will never miss it"; and because they don't realize that shoplifting is a crime.

In fact, many teen-agers become confused or indignant when apprehended, and are shocked when they learn they must appear before a judge. Few understand the severe consequences of being caught stealing, such as the possible harmful effects a criminal record may have on entering college or in applying for a job.

To combat the onslaught of thievery, merchants have taken action on a number of fronts. They have hired security personnel, both uniformed and in plain clothes. And they have employed such deterrent devices as two-way mirrors, closed-circuit television, and sensitized tags on store merchandise. All of this, of course, causes merchants to raise prices that must be paid by honest shoppers.

In many areas, communitywide anti-shoplifting educational programs, sponsored by stores, police and merchants' groups, are held annually.

Experts are in agreement, however, that the most effective key to curbing the teen-age shoplifting problem is in the home. They contend that too many parents are too permissive, overprotective of their children, or are just apathetic and don't care.

But perhaps the ultimate answer to this billion-dollar-a-year problem lies with the teen-ager. It boils down to a simple question: is the spur-of-a-moment temptation to steal something worth the risk of permanently damaging a future life?

CAUGHT IN THE ACT

It was a few minutes after four on a Saturday afternoon, when Janet entered O'Brien's Department Store. As usual, it was crowded with shoppers, the last rush before the dinner hour. O'Brien was one of the nicest stores in town. It wasn't the largest, and it didn't have the variety of goods that the big chain stores offered, but it carried an attractive, if somewhat expensive, line of products that appealed to Janet and her parents.

Janet is from what you might call an average to upper middle-class family. Her father is a marketing executive with a medium-sized industrial company and makes more than $25,000 a year. Her mother is very active in local community affairs: vice-president of the women's club, on the board of directors of the high school parents' organization, and a Sunday-school teacher. Janet's older sister, Teresa, is a freshman at the state university, and her younger brother, Robby, is in the eighth grade.

Janet herself is fifteen, and nearing completion of her sophomore year in high school. She has long, brown hair, down to her shoulders, and is just a little overweight. But she has a pleasant face that is often creased with a smile, and she has a small circle of close friends with whom she has grown up.

She has no material problems. She gets a decent allowance from her parents, and she works part-time during the summer. And if she has a special need for something, such as a prom dress, there is always money available. Nevertheless, Janet thinks she has some problems. Her parents expect too much of her, she feels. Teresa is a brain, and Janet is not getting marks as good as her sister did in high school. Her mom and dad always seem to be down on her, threatening that she won't be able to get into the college she wants unless there is some drastic improvement in her grades.

This causes some anxieties in Janet. It causes her to overeat at times. It causes her to rebel, too. She has yelled back at her parents, and has been punished. So, mostly, she has held her anxieties in. But she has never been in any real trouble.

Oh, she got caught drinking beer at Greg's keg party last summer; so did a lot of her underage friends. And she had missed some curfews, getting home later than her parents liked. But that was no big deal.

Janet walked across the front of the store and stopped to pick through some scarves that were marked down on sale to half price. Then she wandered over to the cosmetics counter and looked at the new shades of lipstick. She put down a tube she was holding as a clerk approached her and asked, "May I help you?"

"No, thanks," Janet said, half smiling, and walked off. She went down the aisle, turned up another, and stopped at the jewelry section. The tray of wristwatches in the glass-enclosed case caught her eye. One particular watch with a bracelet-like band was especially appealing.

"Could I show you something in particular?" another salesperson inquired.

"Yes," said Janet. "I'd like to see that tray of watches."

"Certainly," the clerk replied, lifting it out of the case and placing it on top of the counter.

Janet fingered several watches, picking up one after another and then replacing it.

Just then a woman on the other side of the counter, holding up a pair of earrings, motioned to the clerk.

"I'm in a hurry, young lady," she said. "Could you ring these up for me."

The clerk turned to Janet and said, "Excuse me for a minute. If you see something you like, I'll be right back."

Janet nodded as the clerk left and went over to the woman.

Suddenly, Janet felt a burning, scary sensation in the pit of her stomach. Her eyes darted nervously to the right and left. There were people in the aisles, but no one was paying any attention to her. She looked at the clerk, who was partially hidden from view by a post as she tried to find a small box for the woman's earrings.

Janet could almost feel her blood pumping faster as she picked up the watch she had admired most and held it near the edge of the counter. She looked around her again, first one way, then the other. No one was watching. Then she brought her pocketbook, which had an open top, up to the side of counter and slid the watch into it from the counter top.

She put the pocketbook's strap over her shoulder,

looked around again quickly, and then started to walk off. She was nervous as she turned back up the aisle and headed toward the front exit.

The watch was not the first thing Janet had taken from O'Brien's. The first thing had been some nail polish about three years earlier. She had taken it on a dare from her friends, Kerry and Diane. They had shown her how easy it was to take things without paying for them, by doing it right in front of her. It was like a game, they had told her. Everyone did it.

Over the next couple of years, Janet had taken other things . . . cologne, beauty soap, compacts. She had even slipped some records under her winter coat.

She didn't have to take them. She had the money to pay for them. But it was "the" thing to do. She had never before taken anything as expensive as this watch, but she knew that Kerry and Diane and her other friends would be impressed when she showed it to them.

She was just a few feet from the door when a matronly-looking woman in her fifties stepped in front of her.

"Just a minute, young lady," the woman said to Janet.

"Wha . . . what?" Janet stammered. "Are you talking to me?"

"Yes I am," the woman said. "Would you please come with me to the office?"

Janet felt the blood drain from her face, and her mouth was suddenly dry. She had trouble catching her breath.

"There must be some mistake," Janet finally managed to say. "I'm in a hurry, so would you please let me by?"

The woman didn't budge. Janet was near panic.

"Listen, young lady," the woman said, with a touch of iciness in her voice. "You can either come with me peacefully, or I can handcuff you right here and lead you to the office. Now what will it be?"

Perspiration beads popped out on Janet's forehead. She could feel that other shoppers, coming in and out of the front door, were stopping to see what was going on. She wished she could turn invisible or disappear.

The woman walked Janet briskly back up the main aisle. Janet went along, almost in a fog.

She felt humiliated. What if someone I know sees me, she wondered. This is awful.

The woman turned right, down an aisle past the front section, and walked with Janet through a door marked "Employees Only." She didn't say a word. They walked down a narrow hallway to a door that had "Security" in big letters across its opaque window. They went inside.

The room was bare and seemed cold to Janet. A security officer was seated behind a gray metal desk. In back of him was a row of equally drab metal file cabinets. There were two plain wooden chairs in front of the desk.

"Sit down," the woman said. Janet did.

"Please put the merchandise you took on the desk," the officer said.

"What merchandise?" Janet asked. "What are you talking about? Why have you taken me here? I haven't done anything."

The officer stared directly into Janet's eyes. She had trouble looking at him.

He sighed, and then said, "It will be a lot easier on all of us if you will just put the merchandise you took on the table."

"She has a watch in her pocketbook," the woman said.

Janet's mouth dropped open a little as she looked at the woman standing by her chair.

"Ms. Evans is a security officer here," the other officer said. "And she saw you take the watch."

"But she doesn't have a uniform," Janet said. "She looks just like a shopper."

"She's a plainclothes security officer," the officer answered. "Please, young lady. Let's don't make this more unpleasant than it already is."

Janet felt trapped. In a flash of temper, she reached into her purse, took out the watch, and half threw it on the desk.

"Here," she snapped. "Here's your old watch. As if O'Brien's would miss it anyway. How much is it? I have ten dollars I can put down on it and I can pay you the rest next week. Can I go now?"

The two officers looked at each other. The man shrugged his shoulders and said, "I'm sorry, but that won't be possible."

"What do you mean?" Janet shrieked. "I've offered to pay for the watch."

"Shoplifting is a crime, young lady," the officer said. "It is stealing, the same as if you had broken through a window and taken that watch after the store was closed.

"This watch cost $59.95. Anything over $50 in this state is a felony, not a misdemeanor. It leaves us no choice. Even if we wanted to let you pay for the watch and go, we couldn't. The store's policy is to prosecute all felonies. There are no exceptions."

The words stung Janet sharply. The resentment she had displayed only a moment before rapidly turned to fear.

The officer took a paper form from the top drawer of his desk, grabbed a pen, and looked at Janet. "What is your name?"

A wave of emotion broke over Janet. Her eyes welled with tears.

"Janet . . . Janet Stuart."

"May I see some identification, please," the officer asked. "A driver's license, school ID card, or social security card."

Janet fumbled in her purse and finally found her school ID.

"Please, please don't call my parents," Janet begged, as she sobbed. "I'll do anything you ask if you don't call them."

"We have no choice, Miss Stuart," the officer said. "We have to call them."

He filled in Janet's name, address, birth date, social security number, parents' names and places of employment on the form.

Janet continued to cry.

"Does this mean I'm going to jail?" she asked.

"That's for the judge to decide."

She buried her face in her hands and her shoulders shook.

The officer dialed her home number.

"Hello. Mrs. Stuart? This is Officer Hamilton, chief of security at O'Brien's Department Store."

Janet could hardly believe all this was happening to her, as the officer told her mother the whole story. It was obvious from the conversation that Mrs. Stuart was shocked at what she was hearing.

"If Mr. Stuart is home, either he or you could meet

Janet at the police station. Yes, that's right. Just ask for the juvenile officer there, and they'll take you to Janet."

The officer then called the police.

As they waited for them to arrive, a statement of Janet's theft of the watch was typed up.

"We'd like you to read this over, make sure it's correct, and then sign it," the officer said. "You don't have to sign it, but we'd like you to."

Janet signed it.

A few minutes later a policewoman walked into the small office. She looked at Janet, then read the signed statement.

"I'm Officer Wolinsky," she said. Then she read Janet her legal rights, just like it's done on television.

The officer then took the watch and statement and said to Janet, "Come with me, please."

Again, shame and embarrassment swept over Janet as they walked back through the store. She wanted to run and hide, or cover her face. She felt as if everyone in the store had stopped and was staring at them.

Fifteen minutes later, at the police station, Janet felt even more humiliation. She was fingerprinted and photographed, and more forms were filled out. She felt like a criminal.

A little later her parents arrived. Officer Wolinsky, Janet, and her parents all sat at a table in a tiny room.

The policewoman briefed the Stuarts on the procedures that would be followed. Janet could go home with them, under their cognizance. A date would be set for a hearing before the juvenile judge.

Because Janet did not have any previous arrests or a police record, Officer Wolinsky said it was likely that she

might get a suspended sentence with a period of probation, although under state law, she could be sentenced to
up to a year in jail.

Janet's parents were silent most of the time. They just
listened. They were dumbfounded, and each time they
glanced at her, Janet felt as if her body were shriveling.
She could sense the hurt they were enduring because of
her.

At last, the discussions were over, and Janet and her
parents left the police station. As they stepped onto the
sidewalk outside, her mother turned to her.

"Janet, darling, why ....?"

A BILLION-DOLLAR PROBLEM

Janet is not fictitious. Janet is not her real name, but she is a real person. The horrifying experience that happened to her is a real-life occurrence that is being recreated by thousands of teen-agers, both boys and girls, every day in every state in America, and throughout the Canadian provinces.

According to the latest estimates, compiled from records maintained by the Federal Bureau of Investigation (FBI), the U.S. Department of Commerce, the National Retail Merchants Association, private security companies, and other sources, about four million shoplifters are caught in the act each year. Roughly half of them are teen-agers.

But even more staggering, say experts of the Insurance Information Institute in New York, as many as 140 million instances of shoplifting occur each year in the United States, again with about half of them committed by young people. Which means, when broken down statistically, that for every person caught shoplifting, there

15

are thirty-four thefts from stores that go undetected, or if detected, where the criminal gets away.

There are no exact national figures on what percentage of shoppers take things from stores without paying, but studies have uncovered some alarming trends. In one such study conducted by a major security firm, five hundred randomly selected shoppers were followed through a New York City department store. Forty-two of them— one of every twelve shoppers—were observed stealing some item from the store. In a similar study in a Philadelphia store, it was one out of eleven shoppers, and in a Boston store, one out of twenty. Other reports, from all parts of the nation, have revealed anywhere from one of every eight shoppers, up to one of every twenty shoplifted.

This epidemic of stealing has become so widespread that the FBI says shoplifting now is one of the fastest-growing forms of larceny in America. The rate of incidence of this crime increased more than 250 percent in the 1960s, and jumped another 76 percent during the first half of the 1970s. It is currently rising at an annual rate of 20 percent.

There are varying estimates of just how much is taken illegally each year from the more than two million retail outlets in the United States. The Department of Commerce says that retail businesses—including clothing and department stores, drugstores, food stores and variety shops—lose more than $8 billion a year to crime. Of this figure, roughly one-third is attributable to burglaries and robberies and transportation thefts.

The other two-thirds, or more than $5 billion, is caused by "internal theft." About 60 percent of this is due to employees who steal from the stores where they work.

The remaining 40 percent, or $2 billion a year, is charged to shoplifting. Half of this—more than $1 billion a year —is taken by teen-agers. And only a very minute portion of stolen goods is returned. For example, the J. C. Penney Company, one of the nation's largest chain stores, reports that it recovers less than 1 percent of the value of shop-lifted items.

Also sharply on the increase is the average amount of goods taken during each shoplifting incident. The average today ranges from $14 to $50, according to the Metro-politan Washington Board of Trade's Retail Bureau.

"Twenty years ago, the figure was almost infinitesimal by comparison," says a spokesman for the National Retail Merchants' Association. "It used to be that teens would swipe a fifty-cent tube of lipstick, a dollar penknife, or a handful of candy or bubble gum. But now it's a big business."

Some representative recent cases from around the country point this out.

☐ In Boston, a seventeen-year-old boy was caught slipping a $6.98 stereo record into his jacket. Police later found eighty-two more records in the trunk of his car, all taken over a short period of time from the same store.

☐ In Detroit, store security officers grew suspicious of the way a teen-age girl "waddled" out of the store. They followed her, and when she got to her car, they stared in amazement as she lifted up her loose-fitting skirt to re-trieve a portable typewriter she had carried between her legs.

☐ Three young girls in North Carolina crammed $72 worth of costume jewelry in popcorn bags in a forty-five-minute spree through two department stores, before being caught.

☐ In Toronto, an eighteen-year-old college freshman tried to walk out of a grocery store after stuffing eight sirloin steaks in a plastic bag inside his overcoat.

☐ Clerks at a department store in Southern California couldn't believe their eyes when they saw a fifteen-year-old girl step out of a dressing room and try to leave the store. She looked as if she suddenly had put on about forty pounds. After she was apprehended, security officers found she was wearing twelve bikini swimsuits under her clothes.

☐ In Williamsburg, Virginia, a teen-age boy ripped a $40 price tag off an artificial Christmas tree, substituted a $6 tag on it, brazenly paid an overworked clerk in a crowded store, and walked away.

☐ In a large department store in Toledo, Ohio, the manager curiously watched one teen-age boy pushing another teen out of the store in a wheelchair. What drew the manager's attention was a large lump under the blanket covering the legs of the boy in the wheelchair. A security guard followed them outside and discovered a $300 portable color television under the blanket.

All of this, of course, is enormously costly to merchants and, eventually, to consumers. According to the National Retail Merchants Association, the cost to specialty shops due to thefts is 2.7 cents for every dollar in sales, and for larger department stores, the loss is 2.1 cents per sales dollar.

"This is a substantial amount," says the National Retail Merchants Association spokesman. "Many people have the misconception that retailers make a 20- or 30-percent profit. This is simply not true." In one detailed study conducted in the Midwest, for example, teen-agers believed merchants made an average of 24 cents profit on every sales dollar. The spokesman says this belief may come from the fact that merchandise may be marked up 30, 40, 50 percent or more over cost, which may be the case. But most people do not take into account overhead costs, such as employees' salaries, store rent and maintenance, taxes, cost of utilities, transportation costs, even the cost of security. If the shoplifter is not apprehended and the stolen merchandise returned, the loss ultimately comes from the profit.

"Actually, the profit figure for retailers is more like 2 or 3 cents for every sales dollar, not 30 cents," the spokesman says. Most merchants contend that for every $20 stolen, they must sell $1,000 worth of goods just to make up the loss. With supermarkets, the profit margin is even smaller, generally one percent. Thus, grocery stores must sell $2,000 worth of products to make up a $20 shoplifting loss.

Some stores cannot afford such losses. Studies show that small businesses suffer an impact from crime three times greater than larger firms with annual sales of $5 million or more. Unfortunately, these small businessmen and women are the least able to absorb such losses, nor can they afford the high cost of overhead required for extensive protective measures.

Many retail stores, particularly small specialty shops and boutiques, have been forced out of business because of the high costs of shoplifting. The United States Small Business Administration reports that criminal losses now cause 30 to 40 percent of all small business failures.

The owner of one clothing store in Houston, Texas, figured it cost him over $25,000 a year for security protection to hold down theft. It was more than he could afford and he closed his store. A general rule of thumb many small merchants use is that they can afford one store detective or security guard for each $1.5 million they do in annual sales. But what of the stores and shops that sell less than this amount? They must do with part-time protection, or no protection at all, and often become open targets for shoplifters.

In shopping malls and downtown areas in small towns and large cities across the country, it is common today to see uniformed security guards posted at or near the door. Other security people are dressed in plain clothes to appear as shoppers. Security equipment—everything from closed-circuit television to alarm sounding tags—costs merchants hundreds of millions of dollars to install and maintain.

With such a small margin of profit on sales, merchants have only one way of affording such costs for security caused by increased theft. That is to consider shoplifting as another operating expense and to pass on such costs to the consumer in the form of higher prices.

In a nationwide survey covering a large portion of the country's self-service department stores, the Mass Retailing Institute reported that: "American families each pay a hidden tax, probably exceeding $150 a year, because of merchandise stolen from stores."

Who eventually pays for the $1 billion teens shoplift every year? The average American consumer, including teen-agers.

You pay!

PROFILE OF A SHOPLIFTER

There is no such thing as a "typical" teen-age shoplifter.

Young thieves, rather, come in every size, shape, age, religion, color, sex, and from every kind of family background.

While the estimates vary somewhat, there is a general consensus among law enforcement and security officials that the overwhelming majority of all shoplifters, including teen-agers, are amateurs. That is to say, they are not professional thieves who make their living from stealing from stores, or kleptomaniacs who steal because of a sickness.

Some experts believe that 95 percent of all shoplifters are amateurs. However, they also feel that professionals, also known as "boosters," may account for 10 percent or more of all shoplifting losses, because they steal more items and more expensive items. Only a small percentage of boosters (no exact figures are available) are believed to be teen-agers.

Professional shoplifters often work in pairs and use sophisticated equipment, such as wrapped packages with false bottoms, hollowed-out books, oversized bloomers and bras, and coats with extra-large, hidden pockets, fitted with special hooks. They are also masters of psychological effects. Often, one partner will purposely divert the attention of a clerk, or even cause an attention-getting disturbance, so the other can steal undetected. They know which stores have tight security and which ones don't, and they know when to strike; generally when a store is crowded, or near closing time when clerks are tired or hurrying to tally up the day's sales.

Kleptomaniacs also comprise only a very small percentage of all shoplifters, probably well under 5 percent. These people, including relatively few teens, steal compulsively. They are sick, often feeling an all-consuming urge or desire to take things indiscriminately. In some cases, they are not even consciously aware of what they are doing, and if apprehended, they express shock or amazement at what they have taken. There are cases on file of teen-age kleptomaniacs who have been driven by impulse a dozen or more different times a day to steal. And in many instances, they are casual in committing the act, unconcerned by security measures. Consequently, they are much easier to catch than professionals are. Rather than arrest and punishment, kleptomaniacs need professional psychiatric treatment to overcome their illness. Studies also have shown that drug addicts account for only a minute percentage of shoplifters.

Together, boosters, kleptomaniacs, and drug addicts make up such a small percentage of the total number of shoplifters that merchants and security people do not concentrate their efforts on them. It is the amateur thieves, who do perhaps as much as 95 percent of all shoplifting, that cause the primary concern.

And while these amateurs are not as skilled in the professional techniques of stealing, they are, nevertheless, difficult to apprehend, because there is no standard pattern or profile in which they can be categorized.

Amateur teen-age shoplifters include kids from ghettos as well as from wealthy families. Strangely, family background seems inconsequential. Sons and daughters of policemen, lawyers, doctors, politicians, congressmen and congresswomen, civic leaders, ministers, and even store owners have been caught shoplifting.

Experts do agree that most teen-age shoplifters can afford to pay for what they steal. In fact, studies have shown that roughly 75 percent of teens who steal from stores come from families with average or above-average incomes. And a substantial majority of teens apprehended while shoplifting were found to have enough money on them to pay for the item or items they took.

In researching for his book, *The Psychological World of the Teenager,* Dr. Daniel Offer, acting chairman of the Department of Psychiatry at Chicago's Michael Reese Hospital, discovered that many youthful shoplifters came from stable homes and, generally, were successful in their schoolwork and personal relations.

Rough sketch lines of a "typical profile" of a shoplifter emerge from a number of regional studies.

Bob Harry, vice-president of Stores Mutual Protective Association, analyzed 4,000 shoplifters apprehended in six large New York City stores during a six-week period. He found that 66 percent of those caught, two of every three, were under twenty years of age. Of these, 36 percent were under sixteen years old.

In a 1974 study in the metropolitan Washington, D.C. area, 49 percent of apprehended shoplifters were in junior or senior high school. Another 10 percent were high school dropouts. In a Hawaii study of 196 confessed shoplifters, the most prevalent age group was between fourteen and seventeen years old.

Most studies indicate that more teen girls steal than boys. In one large-scale survey conducted by the Mass Retailing Institute, data was compiled on shoplifters apprehended in 1,188 large discount department stores. Fifty-three percent of those caught were under eighteen, and 58 percent were girls.

If there is such a thing as an "average" or mean age of the teen-age thief, it is likely to be sixteen for girls, with the most dangerous ages being fifteen to seventeen; and thirteen for the boys, with the most dangerous ages ranging from twelve to fifteen. But the age range of young shoplifters is by no means confined to these age groups. Each year countless thousands of pre-teens are apprehended. In fact, one Chicago psychiatrist says that many children begin stealing in stores at about age ten.

There are no particular geographical clues to the typical teen-age shoplifter, either. According to the FBI's annual report, *Crime in the United States,* and other studies, the incidences of shoplifting are fairly evenly spread in all major areas of the United States. The same is generally true in Canada, too.

While many people assume that shoplifting is more common in the inner cities of large urban areas, where there are often poverty pockets and large minority populations, this is not true. Store thefts are equally spread among these areas and the more affluent suburban regions. There does seem to be a statistical drop in the rate of shoplifting crimes in rural areas, however. Some sociologists believe this may be because teens are more likely to be familiar with merchants and store personnel, reducing the "impersonal element" that is more common in cities and suburbs.

What do teen-agers mostly steal from stores? Again, the range varies greatly—from candy bars to color television sets. According to a detailed student study conducted in the greater Boston area in the mid-1970s, the items most commonly taken were jewelry, cosmetics, records, and small leather goods, such as purses and wallets. "These are favorites of teenage shoplifters, who want them for personal use," the study report stated.

The next "most popular" group included sportswear, dresses, sweaters, blouses, teen-age outerwear, and men's furnishings. The report said these were favorite targets of young thieves, and well up on the "wanted" list among shoplifters of all ages.

Lingerie, gloves, hosiery, and handbags were described as "useful, and often expensive accessories for all kinds of thieves." Larger, more costly items, such as sporting goods, cameras and camera equipment, small electrical items, tools and other hardware items, reported the Boston study, were "more often taken by the male shoplifter and the professional, but attractive to many thieves."

William Meehan, vice-president in charge of loss prevention at the Korvettes chain of stores, says teen-agers mostly take things they like, such as costume jewelry, clothing, cosmetics, leather goods, sunglasses, and records. "Records represent one of our biggest single shoplifted items," he says.

In another report of seven boys, aged thirteen to fifteen, in a Midwestern city of 125,000, as noted in the book, *Juvenile Delinquency* by Ruth S. Cavan, the following was learned: The boys shoplifted over a period of several

days from two drugstores, two department stores, a
sporting-goods shop, and an office supply store.

During this spree, they took a crowbar, hair tonic, playing cards, gloves, magazines, ice cream, candies, comic
books, wallets, staplers, cigarettes, padlocks, gum, flash-
lights, batteries, cigarette cases, peanuts, shirts, film, and
a wall soap dispenser.

In most cases, the studies showed, teen-agers preferred
to steal items from the main floors of stores, and the
nearer the merchandise was to exit doors, the better.

In the Hawaiian study, based on interviews with 196
confessed teen-age shoplifters, most of the young people
involved were very selective in choosing merchandise to
be stolen, and in choosing stores from which to steal.
Personal items seemed to be preferred, with the reasoning
being that the items were needed and they "wouldn't be
missed by the store."

There even are definite patterns to the *times* when
shoplifting is most prevalent—the hours, days, and sea-
sons. For example, almost every detailed study that has
been conducted regarding shoplifting habits concludes
that more thefts occur on Saturdays, followed by Fridays
and Thursdays. The least number of thefts occur on
Tuesdays and Wednesdays.

There are many reasons cited for this, the most common being that Saturday is usually a store's busiest day
and clerks are occupied by other shoppers, and that it is
not a school day.

Further study data indicate that most shoplifting occurs between the hours of 2:00 and 7:00 P.M. In the
New York study, analyzing 4,000 shoplifting apprehensions, the statistical breakdown was as follows: 47 percent, or nearly half of all thefts, took place between 2:00

and 6:00 P.M.; 20 percent after 6:00 P.M.; 14 percent between noon and 2:00 P.M.; and only 8 percent before noon. Again, the logic behind these numbers is that stores are usually busiest in the afternoon hours, especially in the time periods just prior to closing. Stores are least busy in the morning hours, particularly in the time period just after opening. That is why so few shoplifting incidents occur in the morning.

Merchants and security experts from coast to coast generally agree that most store thefts are committed during the fourth quarter of each year, predominantly in the Christmas shopping period.

Gerald Lauritzen, director of the Southern California Stores Protective Association, says that 35 to 40 percent of any year's total losses from shoplifting occurs in the final three months of each year. He believes this is the direct result of increased shopping traffic during the holidays.

And an article in the J. C. Penney Company employees' newspaper reported, "For an alarming number of Americans, getting into the Christmas spirit means taking, not giving. Shoplifters seem to come out of the woodwork during Christmas to take advantage of the increased traffic in the stores—traffic they believe provides them more camouflage than at any other time during the year."

An interesting insight into how frequently teen-agers commit shoplifting as opposed to other types of offenses evolves from one study of unrecorded juvenile delinquency made at several high schools in Western states. High-school students were asked to fill out questionnaires that listed twenty-one separate offenses, ranging from skipping school to gang fights.

Nearly 61 percent of the boys participating said they

had shoplifted. In fact, only three other offenses in the list of twenty-one drew higher percentages. They were: fistfighting with another person, 81 percent; driving a car without a driver's license or permit, 75 percent; and hunting or fishing without a license (or violating other game laws), 63 percent.

More boys had shoplifted than had bought or drank beer, wine or liquor, or had tried drugs. More had shoplifted than had skipped school, had defied their parents' authority, or had damaged property.

The same questionnaire also was given to teens at a correctional school. Here, 92 percent of the boys admitted to shoplifting. The only offenses with higher ratings were skipping school, 95 percent; and fistfighting, 95 percent.

Somewhat surprisingly, only 30 percent of the high-school girls said they shoplifted. The number-one offense cited among the girls was driving a car without a driver's license or permit, 58 percent. This was followed by drinking beer, wine, or liquor, 54 percent; skipping school, 41 percent; and defying parents' authority, 31 percent.

Among girls at a correctional school, however, 78 percent admitted shoplifting. This was topped by skipping school, 94 percent; buying or drinking beer, wine, or liquor, 90 percent; and running away from home, 85.5 percent.

WHY THEY STEAL

Many experts say that ten or twelve years ago one of the principal reasons teen-agers cited for shoplifting was as one means of expression at "getting even" with "the establishment." In the late 1960s and early 1970s, there was much national unrest over the Vietnam War. Students rioted on campuses and in the streets. Several young people were shot by National Guardsmen at Kent State University. Martin Luther King, Jr., and Robert Kennedy were assassinated. It was a time of national unrest and charged with emotions.

As an outlet against the establishment, teen-agers shoplifted heavily from stores—the larger the stores the better. It was one way of displaying a rebellion against a society whose general viewpoints they did not agree with. Stores were one symbol of a materialistic society that, to teens, was more interested in sales and profits than in human values.

But things have changed dramatically over the past few years. The war is over, much of the unrest has eased, and young people are not as expressively rebellious as they were.

Why do teen-agers shoplift today?

Here are some of the most common answers apprehended teen-age shoplifters give:

—"I did it for kicks."
—"Everyone does it."
—"The store will never miss it."
—"I did it on a dare."
—"It's crazy to pay for something when I can take it for nothing."
—"The store rips me off with high prices, so I take things to get even."
—"It was an impulse."
—"It was so easy to take it, I was overcome with temptation."
—"It's like a game."
—"I know they won't do anything to me if I'm caught because I'm underage."
—"My parents wouldn't let me buy it."
—"I didn't know it was a crime."

Stealing for kicks or for the thrill of it seems to be one of the most dominant and most disturbing reasons cited today for the upswing in teen-age shoplifting. Judge Leonard Wolf of Los Angeles, California, calls it "the phenomenon of the teen-age thrill thief." "Most of these kids," he says, "have plenty of money. They steal just for the hell of it—the way they smoke pot."

William M. Drupka, assistant vice-president of corporate security for the Perry Drug Store chain in Michigan, adds: "Dialogues our security people have had with scores of apprehended juvenile shoplifters make it all too clear that young people today generally think of shoplifting as high-spirited fun rather than the risk of a police record and a lifelong stain on their reputation."

One fifteen-year-old girl, observed stealing an imitation pearl necklace from the counter of a New York department store, openly bragged about it later. "It's great fun," she said. "I never think about getting caught, just getting what I want. What's most cool, when you're with other kids, is to take things and walk out real casually. It's like a contest to see who can carry it off the best."

Joseph Giunta, formerly with the Illinois Youth Commission, believes this "fun" angle is at the very heart of the problem. "Kids don't seem to think of shoplifting as a crime, but rather as a game called 'beat the system'," he says. "It never occurs to them that stealing a $30 dress is no different from stealing $30 out of a store's cash register."

An example of how many teen-agers feel about shoplifting occurred in a large department store in the Midwest. A woman security guard saw a young girl, about sixteen or seventeen, take a scarf from a counter and stuff it in her purse. Rather than apprehend her in the store, the guard, dressed in street clothes, followed the girl into the store's coffee shop, where she was met by two of her friends. She pulled the scarf out of her bag and waved it proudly, like a pennant. Then her friends dug into their handbags and produced a bottle of cologne and a pair of pantyhose. All three girls then doubled up with laughter, congratulating themselves on what they had taken.

When the guard later approached the girl who had stolen the scarf, she said, defiantly, "Big deal. As though a store like this couldn't afford it." When the guard asked if she didn't have enough money to pay for the scarf, the girl snapped, "That's not the point. It was such fun to see if we could get away with it. It's being done all the time."

One New York store manager sums up the frustration of retailers all over when it comes to dealing with the attitude of young shoplifters. "In my generation," he says, "if I stole even a piece of bubble gum and the merchant caught me, I'd either be in tears, or pleading with him telling him I was sorry, and asking that he not tell my mother and father.

"But the reactions we get today are incredible. I've had kids laugh in my face after they were apprehended. They say, 'So you caught me, so what?' or 'What are you going to do about it?' I don't care what background they come from, the general attitude of teen-agers today is what's so terrible about shoplifting."

Store managers and security officers agree that when youthful shoplifters are apprehended or arrested now, they are more often arrogant than repentant. And in some cases, the influence of television crime shows is apparent. In Los Angeles, for example, a thirteen-year-old boy caught stealing in a department store told his captors, "I know my rights. I want a lawyer." In Lexington, Kentucky, a preteen shoplifter neither cried nor protested when he was brought into the security office. He merely shrugged and handed the security man the business card of the lawyer who had represented him when he was put on probation just two days earlier—for shoplifting!

Another major reason for teen-age shoplifting is peer pressure. Most of the juvenile judges in the country have heard the lame excuse of arrested teen thieves: "All the other kids do it, so why shouldn't I?" In the Hawaiian study of 196 confessed teen shoplifters, peer acceptance and approval were cited as strong motives for shoplifting.

Alex Ackerman, a California juvenile probation officer, says, "With today's kids, when a practice becomes widespread, it automatically becomes acceptable. Added to this is what we could call the 'I-dare-you' factor. Teenagers just can't be square." And, says Angus Steward, chief of security for the K Mart in Sydney, Nova Scotia, "most teens we have apprehended were on a dare, or trying to live up to the boast that they had not paid for a thing in several months, or that they had outwitted a security detective. Thus, stealing becomes a means of acceptance or status."

"Here," says Dr. Robert Gould, Professor of Clinical Psychiatry at New York Medical College, "peer influence plays an important part. There's a spirit of camaraderie and a sense of danger in outwitting the authorities. There's excitement in getting away with something." "Dares" may even be carried to the extreme where they become part of initiation ceremonies for entrance into high school clubs and sororities. Fifteen girls, all from well-to-do families, were picked up in a West Los Angeles shopping center for shoplifting. They told the police they had to steal $100 worth of merchandise from certain stores, with the price tags still intact, to be accepted into a sorority. And in a wealthy Chicago suburb, security officers at a fashionable department store uncovered a "cashmere club" in which each girl had to steal a cashmere sweater in order to become a member. In the investigation that followed the apprehension of two girls, eight other members were discovered.

Psychologists say another reason for some shoplifting, somewhat akin to peer pressure, involves the literal "buying" of friendship among teens. They point to numerous case histories where boys and girls have stolen popular items and then given them away to others. These teenagers often feel inferior, are often teased or otherwise ostracized by their peer groups, and try to buy their acceptance into the group.

Another key motive for shoplifting, according to a number of studies, is a means of defiance of authority— the authority of society in general, and often, of parents in particular. Dr. Chaytor Mason, a Los Angeles clinical psychologist, says: "Some kids express their dissatisfaction with adult society by taking drugs or running away from home. But many turn to shoplifting, which they think is safer and less radical. They seem to need to prove they don't have to live within the rules and regulations of the adult world. Their parents have made them feel they must assume a submissive role. Shoplifting is a means of expressing for them—a way of saying 'I'm not obeying the rules.' Many times they steal ridiculous things in a desire to defy. A girl, for example, may steal makeup or an uplift bra because her mother won't let her wear them."

Dr. John E. Meeks, director of child psychiatry at the Psychiatric Institute in Washington, D.C., believes shoplifting may be a more hostile act with boys than with girls. "It's a way of saying, 'I don't need you, and you don't have to give me what I want. I'll take it'," he says.

Boys who steal are often angry at their parents. Shoplifting becomes a form of evening up the score with them. This was expressed by a fourteen-year-old Wisconsin boy who was caught shoplifting in his father's sporting goods store. "I felt so rotten about myself," the boy told authorities, "and I was really mad at my father for always

putting me down. This was the best way I could think
of to get back at him."

In an interview with a magazine reporter, a Southern
California high school junior said: "A lot of kids I know
steal just to embarrass their parents, because they feel
their parents don't love them. Their fathers are too busy
with business and golf, and their mothers are all tied up
with social activities. When these kids shoplift, I think
they're saying to their parents, 'I'll get you to pay attention to me, even if you have to come to the police station
to do it.' "

Police officers and juvenile authorities almost unani-
mously agree that parents' inattention to their children is
one of the prime root causes not only of shoplifting, but
of all youth crimes. "One of the first questions we ask
parents called in when their children get in trouble is,
'How much time do you spend with your kids?' " says a
sergeant in the Williamsburg, Virginia, police department.
"All too often, the parents will blush, and look at each
other with blank expressions, or stare at the wall. We
know right away they spend very little time with their
children. We see it all the time."

In the Hawaiian study of confessed shoplifters, researchers found that teen-agers who suffer from emotional
problems, such as deprived social experience or an unhappy family life, seem to get a unique gratification out
of shoplifting. It satisfies a basic need to gain notoriety.
(The study suggests that a child who is deprived of love
often views material goods—candy, clothes, or whatever
—as interchangeable with love and understanding. This
love and understanding, that is, material goods, can be
obtained from a retail store. If the parents stop "paying

off" for any reason, being arrested is an excellent reminder to the parents that they are derelict in their duties. The child is telling his or her parents: "Keep the presents coming or else.")

Less specific to pinpoint, but still a contributing factor to teen-age shoplifting, is resentment of something more intangible—"the establishment." A reformed professional shoplifter, who began stealing when he was thirteen, told store managers at a New York City seminar on youth crime: "Many teens say, 'Well, they [the stores] steal from me indirectly, so I'll steal from them directly.' Some kids feel that as large department stores may sell inferior goods at high prices, this gives them the justification to steal."

On this point, Stan Duba, regional security representative for the J. C. Penney Company comments: "I think it comes down to challenging authority. Teens say to themselves, 'Politicians are corrupt, business is corrupt.' So they challenge authority by stealing from what they perceive as the big, rich, and corrupt business establishment. This, of course, is a fallacy. Actually they wind up stealing from all the honest people who have to pay extra prices on merchandise."

To this end, Dr. Mary Owen Cameron, who wrote the book, *The Booster and The Snitch,* a sociological study of shoplifting in a large Chicago department store, believes that the impersonal aura of the large store contributes to theft. "If you're going to steal, you're much more likely to feel guilty if you personally know the victim. Youngsters who would never consider taking a friend's watch think nothing of stealing one from a department store."

Students caught stealing books from a Canadian bookstore openly said they felt they were justified to take books as a protest against prices they considered too high. The thought that they were committing a crime never entered the picture. Ironically, the bookstore owner said the price of books rose and fell in direct relationship to the amount of shoplifting that occurred.

There is a growing consensus among many juvenile authorities that young people today follow a less stringent code of honesty than Americans of a generation ago. Dr. Abraham Fenster, chairman of the Psychology Department at New York's John Jay College of Criminal Justice, says, "We have a less intense commitment today to moral values of all kinds." A study of students in Lincoln, Nebraska, noted that teen-agers considered shoplifting a normal part of growing up.

In this regard, the continued rise in teen-age shoplifting again can in part be traced directly to parental attitudes. Many normally law-abiding mothers and fathers unknowingly contribute to the development of delinquent attitudes among their children through examples they set. These usually start at a very early age. Mothers, for example, often take young, preteen children shopping with them. These women may munch grapes from a produce counter, or switch sticks of butter into an oleomargarine box that has a much cheaper price on it, without really realizing that their children are observing them.

Fathers may brag about cheating on expense accounts or on income tax forms, sometimes even brag about how they are getting even with or beating the system. Their children interpret such actions as tacit approval to imitate them. And one of the most convenient ways of doing this is shoplifting.

In some instances, psychiatrists and psychologists

contend that teen thievery is associated with sexual development and the problems this can cause. In his book, *Shoplifting: Its Symbolic Motivation—Crime and Delinquency,* author F. E. Rourke said stealing is motivated at times as a "symbolic sexual gratification." Other experts point to shoplifting as an outlet for sexual frustration in teens experiencing tension during puberty.

Adding to this line of thought, Dr. Meeks of Washington, D.C.'s Psychiatric Institute says: "For girls, shoplifting may be connected with their own budding sexuality. They take things like clothes and cosmetics that make them feel more glamorous, more seductive. Many of them aren't comfortable growing up and becoming sexual women. They may have mothers who try to keep them as little girls, constantly questioning them about their clothes and the boys they go with. Stealing gives them a sense of adventure, of breaking away from their mothers."

Another reason frequently cited as a strong factor in why teen-agers shoplift is, simply, temptation. Twenty or thirty years ago there were few self-service discount stores, and in most department and specialty stores, merchandise was kept behind counters and in glass-enclosed cases. Much of it was, without the help of a clerk, inaccessible.

Today, however, everything is out in the open. Small, easily concealable items such as lipstick and other cosmetic items, wallets, scarves, costume jewelry, paperback books, and other products are easily accessible, often on counter tops or in open sales display areas. To attract customers, many of these are placed near the store front, near doors.

In fact, juvenile court officials and sociologists have criticized merchants for what they call literally encouraging teens to steal by displaying their merchandise on open counters. Even store security officers complain about this. But store managers are caught in a dilemma. Shoppers today have become accustomed to closely inspecting an item before they buy it. This phenomenon has been inspired in large part because of the boom growth of self-service discount stores and chains, which operate much like supermarkets.

Consequently, shoppers may shun stores where merchandise is sealed in cases. They regard them as too impersonal. Says Alec Dean, security director for the T. Eaton Company, one of Canada's largest department store organizations: "If you don't let them [the customers] smell, touch and fondle [the merchandise], they'll go somewhere else where they can. This is a penalty the retailer has to pay."

Shoplifting has triggered a dramatic rise in the product packaging industry over the past few years. Many small items—everything from razor blades to toy cars—now come wrapped in larger plastic and cardboard containers, in an effort to cut down on theft.

Still, the easy accessibility of openly displayed merchandise presents a temptation, especially in stores where there are few visible clerks about, to which teen-agers fall victim. In addition to this, many teen-agers believe stores figure on losing a certain percentage of their goods to shoplifters, so they feel no harm is really being done when they steal.

Ironically, retailers themselves are partly responsible for the upswing in shoplifting, not only through tempting displays, but also by super-hyped advertising campaigns. These are aimed at drawing young shoppers into the stores to buy products, but often the ads backfire and the items are stolen instead. High-pressure advertising themes feature such slogans as, "Everyone's wearing it," "Try it, you'll like it," "Let yourself go," "We are giving it away," and "You deserve a break today."

In effect, these messages are saying to teens, "You need this product; your life is incomplete without it." And many emotional, immature young people, influenced by such hyperbole, respond by taking the items without paying for them, whether in fact they need them or not.

Additionally, store managers say, whenever there is a new clothing or beauty fad, shoplifting goes up. Thus advertising and social pressures cause some shoplifting, especially with girls. If the risks seem minimal, girls may succumb to temptation. Jealous of friends who are well dressed and cosmetically beautified, they will steal to create a similar image for themselves.

There are some other factors that contribute to the overall shoplifting problem, but these are considered to cause a relatively minor percentage of all teen-age thefts. One is that some youngsters have too much time on their hands when they are in store areas, and steal as a lark. An example of this involved a girl in St. Paul, Minnesota, who had to wait twenty minutes each day in a shopping center for a bus to take her home from school. To pass the time, she browsed in stores and, eventually, began taking things. When she was finally apprehended, after several weeks of pilfering, she admitted to having taken twenty sweaters and skirts and several dozen pair of panty hose.

Some young people shoplift out of sheer impatience. They get mad at having to wait at unattended cash registers, or having to stand in long lines, so they just stalk out with the merchandise without paying for it. And a small percentage of teens steal because of a real or imagined grievance against the store or its employees. One sixteen-year-old boy who was fired from a drugstore because he was habitually late to work retaliated by shoplifting small items every day after school. The manager finally had to have him barred from entering the store.

Impulse and experimentation are also cited as initial causes of shoplifting, particularly among preteens and early teens. But many do not repeat this practice after one or two attempts at it. Experts believe chronic shoplifters may be bored and unhappy with their lives and unable to find excitement and satisfaction through normal channels.

Why do teen-agers shoplift? A paper, "Psychology and the Problems of Shoplifting," presented at the Midwest Section of the American Business Association Conference, summed up the reasons: "A number of studies have examined the possible motive behind shoplifting. Adversity and financial problems were found to have little to do with shoplifting. In addition to the temptations of self-service and open display counters, researchers consider alienation, rebellion, peer pressure, moral decline and excitement as major factors contributing to the increase of shoplifting."

5.

THE MERCHANTS DECLARE WAR

It was Friday night and the shopping mall was crowded.

Mark, seventeen and a junior in high school, had come to the mall with three of his buddies. After poking around a little, they had decided to have a soda, but Mark declined.

"Hey, you guys," he said, "I'll meet you in a few minutes. There's something I want to look at in the department store."

Minutes later, Mark was fingering a handsome sport shirt in the store. It was a designer shirt, very nice, but the $19.95 price tag was more than Mark could afford, and more than he would pay for the shirt even if he had the money.

Mark looked around. There was only one clerk in that section of the store at the moment, and he was busy with some customers, showing them some cuff links. Deftly, Mark slipped the shirt, packaged neatly in a transparent light plastic wrapping, inside his jeans jacket, where he held it under his armpit.

As casually as he could, Mark started toward the store

exit, which led back into the mall. As he passed through the open doors, a loud alarm suddenly went off. Mark could feel the hair on the back of his neck rise as the alarm continued. He felt a large knot in the pit of his stomach. He had an impulse to run, but he couldn't get his feet to respond. Everyone in the mall, or at least it seemed like everyone, was staring at him.

Within seconds a clerk from the store and a uniformed security guard came up to Mark.

"Young man, would you please step inside the store with us," the guard said.

"W-w-why?" Mark stammered. "I haven't done anything." He didn't sound very convincing, even to himself.

"Please, young man," the guard persisted.

Mark saw his buddies down the mall as they and a gathering crowd watched to see what was happening. Mark's eyes dropped from them to the floor. He felt totally humiliated.

Inside the store's security office, Mark took the stolen shirt from his jacket and gave it to the officer. He didn't understand what had happened, and the man explained it to him.

"See this tag, here?" he asked, pointing to a white plastic tag about 4 inches (10 cm) long and 1 inch (2.6 cm) wide, attached to the bottom of the shirt. It had a small, knoblike rise at one end.

"This is a sensitized tag," the officer explained. "You can't remove it yourself. Only a clerk can remove it when you pay for the shirt, and then it has to be done by special machine. If the tag is not removed, however, it trips off an alarm the minute you leave the store, because you pass by electronic eyes at the entrance. Once the tag passes those eyes, the alarm automatically is set off."

Mark shook his head. "That almost doesn't seem like it's fair," he said.

"Not fair?" the officer asked. "Son, is it fair for you to steal a $20 item from our store? Let me tell you something. When it comes to shoplifting, all's fair in love and war. And we consider ourselves in an all-out war against shoplifters."

The store pressed charges against Mark, and he was arrested by the police.

This incident is true. It is a scene that is being repeated every day, thousands of times, across the country.

The use of sensitized tags and other electronic systems, as well as the employment of a number of other anti-shoplifting devices—from closed-circuit televisions to better trained store personnel—underscore a definite trend on the part of the nation's merchants. After years of permissiveness and "looking the other way," hoping the problem would disappear, merchants now are getting tough. They are cracking down hard on shoplifters with every means available to them.

It used to be, just a few years ago, that store owners and managers appeared to be almost as embarrassed about catching a shoplifter as was the shoplifter. Merchants were afraid of their store's image. They were afraid if they apprehended and prosecuted a teen thief, the teen-ager's parents and friends would stop shopping at their store. Even when shoplifters were caught in the act, many stores had a policy of trying to reason with them. The kids would be lectured and then let go.

Stores were reluctant to hire and position uniformed guards, for fear that they would inhibit regular shoppers. Clerks were hesitant about checking on customers in fitting rooms, or being oversolicitous in offering to help shoppers.

As a result, young people stole these stores blind. Merchants who adopted these easygoing policies soon found themselves losing money, as well as self-respect. Some of them went out of business.

Shoplifting, in fact, became so widespread, particularly among teen-agers, that merchants began to realize the only effective way they could approach the problem was to meet it head on. They could no longer afford to passively accept shoplifting as a necessary part of doing business.

As a result, merchants across the country have instituted a "get-tough" policy. They have declared war on shoplifters. And with the wonders of modern technology available to them, the merchants have an impressive arsenal of "weapons" that serve as effective deterrents to would-be thieves.

The sensitized tag is just one such weapon, and even it is being improved and updated. One leading national manufacturer of security equipment advertises a tiny piece of foil, smaller than a strip of cassette tape, which forms the "heart" of a revolutionary article surveillance system.

Unlike conventional systems that use a large tag with steel rivets that could deface the merchandise, and must be removed at point of sale, this new strip may be permanently bonded into a clothing label, sewn into a hem or lining by the manufacturer, or applied to an item as a price tag or advisory label.

The encoded label is undetectable by would-be shoplifters or store employees. When an article is properly sold or checked out, the unrecognizable strip is automatically deactivated so that it may pass through monitors at the store's entrance unnoticed. This eliminates the danger of a clerk forgetting to deactivate a tag.

But if someone tries to steal an article protected with this tiny piece of foil, an alarm sounds the instant they leave the store. Further, the encoded strip is impossible to shield with metal foils, the human body, or even when submerged in water. The system is virtually immune to false alarms and completely safe to those working around it.

Another new device being used in department stores is a magnetometer, or metal detector, much like the equipment used for screening passengers at many airports. It can detect the theft of high-value merchandise, such as cameras, tape recorders, and automotive parts. The magnetometer not only alerts its operator to metal objects under the clothing of a person walking past the sensors, but also shows on a display screen the area of the body on which the metal can be found.

To protect items displayed on the tops of retail counters, a device called "Clerk Alert" has been developed. It works this way: An electric current flows through a cable looped through the displayed merchandise. If someone tries to remove one of the objects on display, an alert is sounded.

One of the most commonly used electronic systems is closed-circuit television. With cameras sweeping various areas of stores, security officials can watch what is happening from a bank of TV monitors set up at a central location. Some stores display the cameras openly, and others conceal them. Cameras can be remotely swiveled to zoom in on an area for close-up observation if the operator sees something suspicious. When a suspect is spotted on a camera, the operator can make a videotaped record of the person's moves. If an item is stolen, the operator quickly radios a store detective. A great advantage of this videotape system is the record it provides for use in court. Thus, it not only helps convict shoplifters with visual evidence as proof, but it also heads off any possible countercharges of false arrest.

More and more stores, such as Montgomery Ward and others, are remodeling to install new surveillance posts that blend into the decor. Observation towers are disguised as structural supports. Protruding, two-way mirrors along walls conceal guards who scan the throngs of shoppers crowding the aisles. Large, "fish-eye" mirrors are placed at strategic points where clerks and cashiers can view otherwise hidden aisles.

In addition to the surveillance and electronic devices, stores are employing more security personnel. Many owners and managers feel strongly that the appearance of a uniformed guard acts as a positive deterrent to shoplifting. This is particularly true with smaller stores, specialty shops, and boutiques. Guards often take a position near the entrance of a store, so a potential thief would have to pass directly by them on the way out with stolen merchandise. Chain and department stores also use "plainclothes" security people, who dress in normal street clothes and pose as shoppers.

The director of security for a five-state Western department chain reported at a Department of Commerce seminar on store crimes that a reasonably sized, well-trained security force could prevent forty-five shoplifting incidents for every one shoplifter it caught.

That the combination of visible security guards and

undercover spotters is a strong anti-shoplifting measure is emphasized by two professional shoplifters who discussed preventive measures with New York store managers.

"Knowing that you're being watched and therefore more likely to get caught, will usually make you think twice before trying to steal something," they said.

Understandably, the use of electronic devices and systems and the hiring of security personnel is expensive. It adds significantly to a store's overhead, and cuts sharply into a store's profits. Many stores, especially smaller ones, cannot afford this added cost.

Nevertheless, there are many things even the smallest store can do to help deter shoplifting. The National Retail Merchants Association has a list of suggested anti-shoplifting practices it provides to merchants. On the list:

☐ Keep expensive, high-loss items in a locked showcase, or attached to display racks with chains designed for that purpose.

☐ Use dummy displays or dummy packages on counters.

☐ Arrange small items so they must be unhooked from a stand to be removed.

☐ Station employees so that the entire selling floor can be observed.

☐ Use specially designed mirrors for employees to observe blocked or screened-in areas.

☐ Watch juveniles who enter the store in groups, as well as people carrying large bags or wearing heavy coats.

☐ Alternate hangers on clothing racks so that one hanger faces in and the next one out. This prevents a shoplifter from grabbing an armful of garments off the racks and running out of the store. Customers, however, are not inconvenienced, because they can easily take a single garment down to try it on.

The NRMA also suggests that retailers maintain good housekeeping procedures. Disorganized counter tops, the association contends, only invite a shoplifter. "When arranging your store, try and place counters near the door with merchandise such as toiletries or accessories, under glass. Then caution sales help to keep a close eye on customers when showing items from the case," the NRMA advises.

Even as simple a thing as stapling a sales slip to seal the top of a shopping bag helps deter shoplifting. Self-service discount stores have done this for years, but only recently has this procedure spread to chain stores and department stores.

Many small stores today ask customers to check parcels, shopping bags, and other items at the front of the store as they enter. This cuts down on a common shoplifting ploy: stuffing merchandise into the shopping bag or other package brought in from another store.

Despite a general consensus that many young people, as well as adults, follow a less stringent code of honesty than Americans of a generation ago, security officers find that tighter restrictions in stores are respected. While teen-agers may not have the same high regard for others' property, especially when publicly or corporately owned, they do have respect for people who defend their own property and rights.

Aside from the addition of security personnel and the installation of various antitheft devices, systems, and practices, store owners and managers are further cutting down on teen-age shoplifting by using a simple, but effective measure: they are cracking down hard on thieves caught in the act. Where once they would look the other way, or merely lecture youngsters caught stealing, today they are pressing charges and prosecuting to the full extent of the law.

A few years ago, the world's largest department store, Macy's in New York, only prosecuted one of every four shoplifters. Today they prosecute more than three out of every four. The Jordan Marsh department store chain on the East Coast and in the South now is pressing charges in 90 percent of its shoplifting cases. On the West Coast, the Broadway stores, another large chain, arrest and prosecute with no exceptions.

"Arresting young shoplifters proves very effective," says Bascom Shanks, formerly Broadway's director of security. "It's an unhappy experience for them. They learn their lesson. They rarely come back." In Panorama City, California, the chamber of commerce worked out a concerted program in which all stores agreed to call the police in every teen-age shoplifting case. "We don't get many juvenile snitches there anymore," one chamber official said.

Except for minor thefts and first offenders, Abraham & Straus in Brooklyn prosecutes every shoplifter. That practice and other measures cut apprehensions almost 30 percent in the program's first year. And Alexander's, the huge New York discount chain, has an even tougher policy. It believes in 100 percent prosecution—and it catches 20,000 to 25,000 light-fingered individuals annually, half of them teens.

Lieutenant Frank Jordan, co-director of the San Francisco Police Department's Crime Prevention and Education Unit, says many shop owners have admitted to him that rather than prosecute a shoplifter they have caught, they will simply take back the goods and tell the person to get out and not to come back again.

"We point out that if every store in San Francisco did that, you could do well as a shoplifter," says Lieutenant Jordan. "You could continue to shoplift in hundreds of stores and get a second chance in every store you went to." Jordan recommends that merchants post signs which say shoplifters will be prosecuted, even if it's their first offense. "The signs are a deterrent," he says. "If someone comes into a store and sees that sign, he or she will think twice before shoplifting."

The Metropolitan Washington Board of Trade reports that across the nation, many other stores and shops are instituting similar "get-tough" policies, and they're working. The word gets around that these stores mean business when it comes to shoplifting. Arrested and prosecuted teens spread the word to their friends that the risk is not worth it.

The Small Business Administration advises, "Failure to prosecute first offenders encourages shoplifting. Call the police when you catch a shoplifter. When every merchant in town follows this policy of prosecuting each shoplifter, the word gets around. Amateurs will think twice before yielding to the temptation to pocket a choice item."

Another tactic, strongly recommended by the National Retail Merchants Association, and being employed in cooperative efforts in more and more cities, is an information exchange program. Stores keep files on known or suspected shoplifters and make the information available to other merchants in the city or town. This way, each time a shoplifter is caught, the records can be quickly checked to see if there are any prior apprehensions or arrests.

Also becoming increasingly popular, especially in small and medium-sized towns, are crime prevention clinics, jointly sponsored by local merchants, police departments, chambers of commerce, and other organizations. Police officials, security experts, prosecuting attorneys, and juvenile authorities describe such subjects as how to spot shoplifters, ways to apprehend them, evidence needed to convict them, how to train employees, etc. Often, films are shown, brochures are handed out, and information and experiences are exchanged among participants.

All of the measures discussed here are effective deterrents to shoplifting. But store managers and security experts agree that the front line of defense in the war against theft is a store's sales force. Alertness and courtesy by clerks, officials believe, may be the greatest deterrents to shoplifters.

With other security devices, potential thieves may suspect that they are being watched. But with attentive salespersons, they *know* they are being watched. The simple words, "I'll be with you in a moment," to a customer means good service. But to a shoplifter those words mean "I'm watching you."

A security manager for the J.C. Penney Company says, "Salespersons shouldn't ignore any customers, regardless of whether they look like they're going to buy or not. It's good business to offer assistance to every customer. And since all types of people steal, you never know when you are deterring a shoplifter. Store thieves have to have freedom to steal. They need privacy. By offering to help them find an item, and by being sensitive to shoplifting opportunities, our associates serve notice that they're minding the store. If you take away the opportunity and temptation, you have an excellent chance of taking away the shoplifter's motivation. The surest way to curtail shoplifting is to perform the most fundamental exercise of customer service. Let the customer know you care, and anyone in the store to steal, not to buy, will get the message. No thief wants to risk an easy chance to get caught."

The need for such attention is as true on the main floor of a store as it is in the fitting rooms. Al Frantz of the Insurance Information Institute says, "In a quality men's store, such as Brooks Brothers, every customer for a suit is waited on by a salesperson. The salesperson then accompanies the customer to the fitting room and introduces him to a tailor, who checks for alterations. The customer feels important, and no one has ever been known to leave Brooks with a new pair of trousers under his old."

In the Hawaiian study, apprehended shoplifters admitted that policing restrooms and fitting rooms has significant effects on reducing stealing. "Shoplifters often use restrooms as points of exchange and storage," the study noted. "When fitting rooms become cluttered with garments which have been left by customers, an open invitation for stealing is extended. One store found that by having employees continually cleaning and straightening the fitting rooms, their shoplifting losses were reduced from $40,000 to $4,000 a year."

A number of government agencies, merchants' associations, security firms, and other organizations offer advice to store clerks. For example, in its booklet *Crime in Retailing,* the Department of Commerce says, "Sales people must be alert to any unusual action by shoppers which might indicate an intention to steal. Most customers will

examine an item and decide in a short time whether or
not to buy it. A shopper who lingers unduly over a purchase should be watched carefully. Similarly, salespeople
should be suspicious of a shopper who appears to be
examining merchandise but repeatedly glances around the
department.

"Some theft techniques are not as furtive but are nevertheless difficult to combat. Teen-agers sometimes will
converge in a large group on a particular department and
create an uproar. The salespeople will not be able to
watch all of them, and a theft can be accomplished easily.
When a crowd suddenly appears in any department, an
emergency call should be made to security immediately."

The Small Business Administration, in its booklet, *Reducing Shoplifting Losses,* adds, "Generally, salesclerks
should be alert to persons who wear loose coats or capes
or bulky dresses. They should also watch persons who
carry large purses, packages, umbrellas, and shopping
bags."

Teen-age thieves, say security experts, will give themselves away if clerks know how to recognize the tipoff.
They advise: always look to the eyes. If people appear to
scan the department, to dart their eyes from corner to
corner as if to look for impending danger, they may be
shoplifters. Thieves about to steal rarely look at the
merchandise. Quick movements of the head and hands
are other clues. Clerks are told if they are suspicious of a
customer to watch his or her hands. Jerky movements
of the body and head might suggest concealment of items,
and looking about to see if they are being watched. Also,
an apparently clumsy teen shopper who continually drops
things onto the floor might be dropping them into a bag
placed there for the purpose of stealing.

It has become common practice in most stores, especially the larger ones, to have training sessions for employees. Either the store's security chief, or if it's a small store, a local law enforcement officer, may come in to brief employees on how to deter and spot shoplifters. Many stores also have reward systems for employees who foil thieves. Some pay cash in direct proportion to the amount of merchandise that was taken by an apprehended shoplifter.

"The most effective way to control crime-related losses," the Department of Commerce advises, "is a well thought-out crime-prevention program, managed by a competent director of security with full support of top management. An aggressive director of security will concentrate on offensive techniques rather than reacting to crime and catching the thieves. Crime prevention should be the major emphasis of a security program, since apprehension and prosecution of outsiders is expensive and time-consuming. The costs of prosecution, as well as losses to successful thieves, can be greatly reduced through a well designed crime prevention program. This should consist of four major efforts: management, cooperation, hiring and training, and prosecution."

The days of merchants turning the other way, or merely lecturing or "slapping the wrists" of teen-age shoplifters have, for the most part, passed from the scene. With approximately $2 billion being lost each year to shoplifters, store owners and managers have come to the full realization that they are in an all-out war for survival. And today, they are using every weapon available to them to help win that war.

PREVENTION THROUGH EDUCATION

In recent years, a trend has been developing toward attempting to prevent juvenile shoplifting through comprehensive, widespread educational programs. Prevention is much preferred over apprehension and prosecution by everyone—merchants, security officers, and juvenile authorities.

The basic thrust of these well-planned and well-organized campaigns is to get the message across, forcefully and directly, to teens that shoplifting is not only dumb, it is a serious crime for which they may suffer consequences far greater than they realize. Information is designed to reach teen-agers telling them that they may endanger their own future careers and happiness by yielding to the folly of shoplifting.

One key idea behind such informative programs is the widely held belief that the great majority of young people who steal from stores have no real conception of the serious consequences they may suffer when caught. To get the message to teen-agers, concerted, community-wide campaigns, sponsored by merchants, police, and other organizations, are being conducted from coast to coast. The information is being broadcast over public service "spots" on radio and television, in both editorial and advertising coverage in newspapers and magazines, through school and youth organization presentations, through billboard advertising and store displays, and a host of various other means.

As early as 1967, the National Retail Merchants Association, recognizing the need to communicate directly with young people, published an educational pamphlet called *Teenagers Beware: Shoplifting Is Stealing*. Over the years, the NRMA has distributed several million of these pamphlets to thousands of cities and towns throughout the United States.

One of the first municipalities to build an educational program around the booklet was Champaign, Illinois, in 1967. "We had to do something," recalled David O. Webb, then general manager of Champaign's largest department store. "The teen-age shoplifters were costing us $50,000 a year—a good chunk of our profits." Webb sent for the NRMA pamphlet and read it carefully. He was surprised to learn that what were considered harmless shoplifting pranks could actually ruin the lives of teen-agers who didn't realize that stealing for kicks or any other reason could earn them a permanent criminal record.

Webb assembled a committee of local business people and educators, and they rewrote the booklet to conform with Illinois law and their community situation. The new committee had 12,500 copies printed and distributed them to every high-school and junior-high student in town. The handout was accompanied by a massive promotional push in the local newspapers and on Champaign's radio and television stations. Anti-shoplifting billboards went up and posters were displayed in stores all over town.

"Our hope was that the kids would take the pamphlets home for their parents to see," says Webb, "and they did. Adults and teen-agers came up to me and said, 'I never knew it was like this.' And, for the first time, many of our merchants got tough about prosecuting teen-age shoplifters."

The program worked. "It's hard to believe what happened," said Lt. Delmar Dawkins of the Juvenile Division of the Champaign Police Department. "Before the campaign, in an average week we could always count on seven to ten cases of juvenile shoplifting. After the campaign it dropped down to only two or three cases a week."

The program was so successful that it was continued as an annual event, running for two to three months every fall, just before the holiday shopping season. A youth advisory board was added, and the literature and anti-shoplifting talks were extended to elementary-school children. More than 30,000 Champaign children, starting in the fifth grade, now get the word.

"Since we began the program, shoplifting has been cut by 40 percent," says Lieutenant Dawkins. "For the first time, kids are learning what can happen to them."

Two years later a similar program, with the same purpose but using different techniques, was successfully launched in Milwaukee, Wisconsin. The Milwaukee Retail Controllers Association asked popular local disc jockeys to speak, in person, to teens at the city's public and private schools. In six weeks, 57,000 youngsters were reached.

One of the DJs, Chuck Bailey, remembers, "I talked to the kids in their own language, without trying to be too cute. The main point that I hammered home was that shoplifting is a crime, not a game, and that they could ruin their lives by stealing. Later, a lot of them came up to me and said, 'Gee, Mr. Bailey, I just never realized that shoplifting is actually stealing.'"

The Milwaukee group followed up the school visits by distributing thousands of the NRMA pamphlets. Consequently, area stores reported shoplifting declines of from 10 to 50 percent.

Noting the success of these programs, groups in San Diego, Los Angeles, Pittsburgh, Baltimore, Kansas City, Boston, Dallas, and many other cities and smaller communities began campaigns of their own. Some examples:

☐ Detroit: Robert T. Marquart, former executive vice-president of the Greater Detroit Retail Merchants Association, reported an anti-shoplifting campaign going to all the public and parochial schools in the area. "We provide antishoplifting tapes to the local media, to run as public-service announcements," Marquart said.

☐ Houston: The Retail Merchants Association is making extensive use of media, including radio and television public service ads and education campaigns in schools, as part of its campaign.

☐ Denver: The K Mart in Denver sponsors programs at which young inmates of the Colorado State Penitentiary urge teen-agers to keep away from all types of "smaller" crimes, such as shoplifting and vandalism, since they often lead to involvement in more serious crimes.

☐ Cleveland: Craig S. Clark, security director of the May Company in Cleveland, says: "We've experienced a downtrend in shoplifting. We put on programs in area schools for eight-, nine- and ten-year-olds which include slides and demonstrations about how store personnel are

trained to catch shoplifters. Our school program is geared
to preventing the crime and our open acknowledgment
of our surveillance techniques has cut shoplifting. No
doubt about it."

☐ Michigan: Jack Robinson, president of Perry Drug
Stores, Inc., started a "Shoplifting Is a Crime" campaign
aimed at young people in all thirty-three of the Michigan
communities in which the company operates a total of
forty-six stores. "Our objective is to curtail shoplifting to
an absolute minimum, and to, hopefully, at the same time
impress upon youngsters that they do irreparable harm
to themselves when they shoplift because it can bring
them police records that will cost them dearly for the rest
of their lives," Robinson says.

Men's Wear Magazine recently reported: "During
1977, merchants launched formal campaigns against
shoplifters, advertising within their stores that shoplifters
would be prosecuted to the full extent of the law. Police
authorities have co-sponsored many of these campaigns,
and have also been instrumental in persuading young
people through community service programs on the folly
of shoplifting for kicks."

In stores in virtually every state in America and every
province in Canada, shoplifting posters, often depicting
harsh penalties, are openly displayed on walls, posts, and
counter tops. Merchants associations and chambers of commerce run anti-shoplifting ads in local newspapers. One
such ad, sponsored by the Williamsburg, Virginia, Chamber of Commerce, carries the headline, in bold capital
letters: "IS THERE A THIEF IN YOUR FAMILY?" It
goes on to say: "Shoplifting is stealing. Stealing may prevent future employment and licensing in some professions

and occupations. Shoplifters are thieves. Shoplifters raise prices. Join the fight against stealing."

Many community-service and other organizations offer free advice and aid to help prevent shoplifting. The International Lutheran Laymen's League, for example, has run an ad in national publications under the headline, "Shoplifters go to jail!" The ad states, "Know someone who steals? Give our free 'Danger, Hands Off!' book. Policemen, juvenile officers, youth groups, teachers, store executives use its message to help shoplifters stop."

One of the most innovative educational programs aimed at reducing shoplifting has been set forth in the state of Idaho. To draw dramatic attention to the seriousness of the problem, Vicki Patterson, project director for Idaho's Anti-Shoplifting Program, sponsored by the Idaho Retailers' Association, came up with a novel approach.

She went on a shoplifting spree. In four hours, she stole almost $400 in merchandise from twenty-two different stores in a Boise mall. Employees of the stores had not been alerted and were unaware of the thefts.

The following day, Ms. Patterson conducted a seminar on shoplifting for 109 employees of the stores in the mall. They were shocked when she displayed the assortment of stolen goods before them. She followed this by showing anti-shoplifting films, discussing apprehension and prosecution technicalities, and leading question-and-answer sessions with a judge, a prosecuting attorney, and a police official.

Such seminars are presented in all areas of the state where there is a concentration of population, with prosecution of shoplifters usually showing an increase after a presentation. This inventive method of getting the retailer's attention has proved to be very successful, and is only one phase of the campaign, which is aimed at reducing the $50,000 a day that Idaho retailers lose to shoplifters.

A second phase of the program is directed at the state's school system. Seminars are annually conducted at all elementary, junior high, and high schools. School resource officers and college criminology students are used to present a program which stresses the cost of shoplifting to retailers and the penalties for shoplifting.

A ten-minute film, starring two preteen-age boys, and narrated by a twelve-year-old, is slanted toward children in grades one through six. Well over one hundred thousand school children have viewed the film, which is repeated on a continuing basis.

Through extensive statewide media coverage, the campaign's third phase attempts to inform the public of the misfortunes of shoplifting. Large newspaper advertisements dramatically tell the story, in many cases followed by editorials and feature stories. Television commercials and radio "spots" are used. Many TV stations show the commercials as public service announcements. In addition, large posters and bumper stickers have given the campaign further exposure.

Idaho prosecutors, juvenile officers, police chiefs, school officials, and business executives all have acclaimed the effectiveness of the four-year campaign.

One of the most successful of all community campaigns is Philadelphia's STEM (Shoplifters Take Everybody's Money). It was begun in the early 1970s when two prominent merchants, Bernard Kant of Gimbels and Frank Veale of Strawbridge & Clothier, organized a twelve-man committee with the Philadelphia Retail Merchants Association to look into the fast-growing shoplifting problem and work out an effective advertising campaign. The committee, in turn, organized STEM, and to give it extra punch, lined up a blue-ribbon advisory board that included then Pennsylvania Senator Hugh Scott and Richard Schweiker, Governor Milton Shapp, himself a businessman, Philadelphia Mayor Frank Rizzo, and a host of other political, civic, and religious leaders.

The committee then hired an advertising agency and asked it to put across two basic messages. One was that shoplifting is no joke, but a serious crime. The committee wanted it known that shoplifters over eighteen could be arrested and those under eighteen could be given a provisional record and go to the police station. The second point was that shoplifting costs everyone money because it raises prices.

From the start, the advertising agency focused on teenagers because they made up the biggest single group of offenders. It was reasoned that such a campaign would have little impact on hardened criminals who try to make a living shoplifting, or on drug addicts or alcoholics who steal to support their habits. But both the committee and the agency felt a multimedia program could change attitudes and behavior of teen-agers who shoplift.

As it was, the agency felt it had an enormous challenge to reach this audience. Area studies showed that most Philadelphia teen-age shoplifters were neither poor nor black, but well-off youngsters, more girls than boys, and more often from white, middle-class, suburban homes. They represented a tough, cynical group to get to.

STEM began by testing ads on students at two high schools. Officials admitted concern that the program could backfire, and become counterproductive, that is, give kids ideas and spur them to steal even more. But the early results proved otherwise; the program could work.

Armed with positive test results, the STEM team approached Philadelphia's media, seeking broad public-service coverage. In the past, anti-shoplifting messages had been sporadic and usually aired at poor times—in the morning or afternoon, or late at night, just before radio and television stations went off the air. This time, after convincing media experts of the immediacy and size of the problem, prime time was given for the running of anti-shoplifting commercial messages.

During the duration of the campaign, television stations ran 550 free "spots," many in prime-time hours, worth $216,000. Radio contributed 6,700 free spots worth another $260,000. Twenty area newspapers ran nearly 60,000 lines of copy during the period, worth approximately $60,000, and outdoor advertising donated another $36,000 worth of unsold space on billboards and on posters on buses, subways, station platforms, and the tops of taxicabs. STEM also printed 200,000 antishoplifting pamphlets for teen-agers, and another 100,000 pamphlets aimed at parents.

The ads avoided preachiness, but drove home a strong, forceful tone. An example: "Shoplifting is no joke. It's a serious crime. No more getting off with a slap on the wrist. Now shoplifters are being arrested and convicted. This means a criminal record. It could keep you out of college. Kill your chances for a decent job. Cause you to get a thumbs-down when you need a loan. Even people who'd never dream of shoplifting are affected. Because shoplifters don't just steal from stores. Since shoplifters cause higher prices, they take everybody's money."

Many ads stressed specific case histories of teens, based on actual arrests.

—"Ken swapped a college education for a $6.50 pair of jeans."
—"Meg just traded her engagement ring for a $6 blouse."
—"Karen exchanged a $2,500 scholarship for a $9.95 pullover."
—"Carol just traded a $100-a-week job for a $3 belt."

To augment the media blitz, STEM representatives met with high-school officials to develop class discussions and school assemblies. The entire program, for the first year, cost less than $100,000.

It is sometimes difficult to measure the success of such a program directly. But in Philadelphia, STEM definitely has made important inroads in reducing store theft. After its first year of operation—at a time when inventory shortages were rising in other cities, Philadelphia merchants reported their own pilferage rates had been cut 20 percent. Further, while overall shoplifting apprehensions rose 8 percent at some of the major department stores, juvenile apprehensions actually dropped 12 percent.

There also were some indirect benefits of the program. Before STEM, merchants had little opportunity to be heard on the shoplifting problem. But after its tidal wave of publicity, judges and policemen showed more concern for the problem. Today, when the stores discuss shoplifting with law enforcement officials, they get a better reception.

Philadelphia has continued the program annually, with increasingly effective results. In fact, STEM has been successful through the years to the point where it is being used as a model program for other parts of the country. Retailer organizations in Maryland, Ohio, Florida, Indiana, New York, New Jersey, Hawaii, Alaska, and other states have adopted ideas and examples from the campaign.

Of all the area community-educational programs—and more cities and towns are adopting them every year— perhaps none is more thorough, more progressive, and more effective than the annual campaign carried out in the greater metropolitan Washington, D.C. area, covering the nation's capital and several surrounding counties in Virginia and Maryland—3,000 square miles (7,770 km) and more than two million people in all.

The campaign is directed by the Retail Bureau of the Metropolitan Washington Board of Trade. "Shoplifting prevention can be achieved only through a combination of hard-hitting anti-shoplifting posters, radio and television spots, newspaper ads, billboard signs, education programs to parents' groups, and to students—from kindergarten through college," says Leonard Kolodny, manager of the Retail Bureau. "Our campaign is a sales promotion," he explains. "However, we are not selling a product. We are selling honesty."

Bureau officials say that anti-shoplifting campaigns can educate and prevent . . . but when all else fails, they recommend following a "hard-nose" policy on the people who steal. They strongly advocate prosecuting all shoplifters, young and old. Yet, the bureau adds, store security personnel, store principals, and law enforcement officials all agree that prevention is more desirable and less costly than apprehension and court prosecution.

The greater Washington area program is a nonprofit public service campaign funded by $50,000 contributed by more than 120 cooperating member companies. Aside from the Retail Bureau's small staff, which works on the campaign part-time, and the payment for annual printing, transportation, and other costs, almost all work is voluntary. An army of hundreds of local law enforcement officers, merchants, school officials, and others volunteer their time and talents to participate. And area television and radio stations and newspapers and magazines provide hundreds of thousands of dollars of free broadcast time and advertising and editorial space.

Here are some of the major components of the Metropolitan Washington Board of Trade's 1977 campaign:

☐ National Transit Advertising donates space for posters on the inside and outside of thousands of metro-buses which travel on major streets and in and out of shopping centers throughout the greater Washington area daily.

☐ Rollins Outdoor Advertising, Inc. provided fifteen giant billboard locations along major suburban highways in the area.

☐ Hundreds of twenty-two-by-twenty-eight-inch (56 cm by 71 cm) cardboard posters, and seven-by-eleven-inch (18 cm by 28 cm) posters, headlining the 1977 campaign slogan, "Shoplifting: a Game for Losers," were printed and distributed in office buildings, government buildings, utility offices, and in every single classroom in the metropolitan area.

☐ Pride, Inc., as a public service, provided space for poster ads on trash receptacles in various business areas in the District of Columbia.

☐ Bumper stickers were widely distributed to merchants, schools, and others.

☐ Full-page campaign ads ran in the *Washingtonian Magazine* and in the *Washington Calendar Magazine*.

Public service anti-shoplifting advertising appeared at least once a week during the three-month campaign in fifty-nine weekly District of Columbia, suburban county, and ethnic newspapers. The area's two largest daily newspapers, the *Washington Post* and the *Washington Star*, each provided a four-hundred-line ad once a week for each week of the campaign, plus various-size ads used as fillers. This printed advertising announced the number of shoplifters arrested during each prior week, to drive home the program's theme. For example, one ad started: "During the week of September 20 through September 27, 3,000 teenagers and adults were arrested in the metropolitan Washington area." (The Retail Bureau asks that publication of any statistics regarding shoplifting in the area be accompanied with the statement that "while shoplifting problems in the metropolitan Washington area appear to be disproportionately high, one of the reasons can be attributed to excellent statistical data maintained by the Retail Bureau of the Metropolitan Washington Board of Trade. Further, anti-shoplifting efforts in this area are annually sponsored by the Bureau from September 15 through December 31, because about 45 percent of all shoplifting losses occur during the fall-holiday season. Statistics nationwide will confirm that a higher percentage of shoplifting occurs at periods of the year when stores are busiest.")

☐ Thirty-second public service spots were aired on forty-three area radio and television stations. The Retail Bureau contacted each station by letter, and an advertising agency doing work for the bureau personally visited every metropolitan area station. Nearly five thousand spots were used during the 1977 campaign.

☐ As in past years, the bureau sent out detailed questionnaires to all member-companies to collect updated figures on shoplifting apprehensions, arrests, convictions, and other meaningful facts about the seriousness of the problem. The information was used for press kits and for material for radio and television interviews with retailers. All area newspapers received anti-shoplifting news releases on a weekly basis during the campaign.

☐ Approximately nine hundred press kits, including up-to-date data on shoplifting and its consequences, were mailed to all of the junior and senior high school and college newspaper editors in the District of Columbia and nine surrounding counties in Maryland and Virginia. Young newspaper reporters were encouraged to interview store owners, managers, and security directors as a follow-up to the press kits.

☐ Every school superintendent in the Washington area was contacted personally and asked to use anti-shoplifting posters on every classroom bulletin board, from kindergarten through the twelfth grade. Teachers were encouraged to devote several periods of classroom time for discussion of the problems and consequences of shoplifting. An "Educator's Guide to Shoplifting Prevention" was made available to teachers. The Retail Bureau also provided volunteer speakers, law-enforcement officials, juvenile authorities, and merchants to speak at special school assemblies.

☐ Educators were encouraged, too, to conduct annual slogan contests at the schools, with recognition for the winning entry, which would be used in the succeeding year's campaign. Previous slogans used have included: "A shoplifter can count on two things: Getting caught and getting prosecuted"; "Shoplifting is dumb. What's that tell you about shoplifters?"; and "Shoplifting is a crime. Everyone wants to be wanted but not for theft."

☐ Parent-Teacher Associations, service clubs, church and fraternal groups, and others were encouraged to view anti-shoplifting films and to hear presentations by retail volunteers.

Kolodny says that each year hundreds of schools, in every single jurisdiction covered by the bureau, request and receive thousands of copies of display material. "While shoplifting is our problem," he says, "schools are also faced with their own thievery problems in libraries, cafeterias, and classrooms. Thus, the various school systems are motivated to prevent their own in-house stealing and, at the same time, educate young people to the consequences of stealing in retail stores."

Members of the Retail Bureau and others who help draft each year's program used resourcefulness, ingenuity, and thoroughness in mapping out plans. In the package that is sent to schools, for example, is a news release titled, "Ideas for Student Involvement." Teachers are shown how to work students actively into the program through classroom discussion. In social studies classes, it is suggested that teachers have students examine current laws and prosecution procedures, and devise new laws which they think are fair. Science classes are asked to study various methods of electronic detection and have members present ideas for new devices.

Students in English and journalism classes are asked to write articles for newspapers on how the shoplifting problem affects the community, or to cover a shoplifting arrest in a news story. For math classes, the bureau suggests that teachers: "To illustrate how shoplifters raise prices, have students set up a 'store.' Divide students into merchants, shoppers, and shoplifters. Have students figure overhead and projected profit and set prices accordingly. After a brief trading period, have merchants assess shoplifting losses and refigure prices accordingly."

Discussion of what makes a person shoplift is advised for psychology classes. How would different people react when apprehended? Would students turn in a peer whom they see shoplifting? The bureau suggests that classes in drama and theater use role-playing to act out a play including recreation of a shoplifting act, apprehension, prosecution, and repercussion. Students would act out the roles of shoplifter, store manager, police, and bystanders.

The bureau also arranges to have plainclothes police officers or retail security directors speak to classes on exactly what constitutes shoplifting, including an explanation of the arrest procedures, interrogation of the thief and fingerprinting. Local prosecutors are available to explain the prosecution procedure and law, and to cover possible long-term consequences of being caught shoplifting. Field trips to visit local police stations or the security departments of major department stores also are arranged.

For its press kits that are widely distributed to the area's media, the bureau each year gets fresh quotes and statements from leading law-enforcement and civic officials. For example, for the 1977–78 campaign Mayor Henry T. Arrington of the city of Seat Pleasant, Maryland, gave this comment: "Teen-agers comprise the largest part of the shoplifting problem. This is doubly unfortunate. One silly impulse on the part of a teen-ager can lead to problems with the law and his or her future getting a job. . . . More shoplifters are being caught. Eighty-nine percent of those caught shoplifting in Prince Georges County last year were found guilty."

And Mayor William E. Hanna of Rockville, Maryland, added: "Most shoplifting is a home grown problem. It is a crime primarily committed by local residents in the community in which they live. Although these people may view shoplifting as a faceless, victimless crime, actually it is like stealing from a friend. They are stealing from local retail merchants, and their actions result in higher prices for their friends and neighbors. Both self-respect and respect for other people and their property are basic to society. If these qualities are to survive, they must be nurtured in our young people."

Inspector Homer A. Boynton, director of Public Affairs for the Federal Bureau of Investigation in Washington, warns: "It is not a large step from pocketing costume jewelry slipped off a counter to dipping into cash registers carelessly left open, to mugging, to armed robbery, to bank robbery. The FBI doesn't want to meet the uncaught shoplifters as criminal ventures increase. But meet these offenders we will, unless they can be persuaded to stop their activities or unless they are stopped by being caught and prosecuted."

John W. Rhoads, Prince Georges County, Maryland, police chief, said, "Our society cannot afford to allow these teen-agers to learn they can steal from stores and go unpunished. I am encouraged to learn that most merchants are willing to take the time to prepare charging documents against shoplifters, and to appear in court as prosecution witnesses. I know this is an expense and inconvenience for merchants, but it is necessary."

Statistically, the Bureau points to a steady and, in fact, dramatic decline in the percentage increase of shoplifting losses each year as a strong indicator of the program's effectiveness. For the 1973 campaign, for example, losses in the greater metropolitan Washington area totaled $345 million—up 46 percent over the previous year. In 1974, however, the losses incurred by shoplifting rose only 8 percent. And the percentage increase has fallen each year. In 1976, the percent increase was down to just 2 percent. At the same time, the increase in shoplifting nationally has gone up at a sharply higher rate. Kolodny is hopeful of soon halting the increase altogether, and starting a decreasing percentage curve.

There are, of course, no statistics to show how much shoplifting crimes and dollar losses would have jumped had there been no annual anti-shoplifting campaign. But many area merchants and law officers believe that without the program, the yearly losses might well have been double or triple the nearly $400 million that was lost in 1976.

The entire metropolitan Washington community appears to be involved and supportive in this anti-shoplifting campaign," says FBI Inspector Homer Boynton, "so I can understand why the shoplifting figures are on the decline. I believe that this campaign could serve as a model to the rest of the country. I hope they will come here for advice."

"Our program is designed to deter the would-be shoplifter from committing this crime," says Kolodny. "With the cooperation we have received from all sectors of the community, retailers are optimistic that our shoplifting losses will be reduced." (Materials from anti-shoplifting campaigns are paid for by retail members of the Metropolitan Washington Board of Trade. It is for their exclusive use only. However, certain materials are available for purchase by individuals or firms located outside the metropolitan Washington, D.C. area.)

A BAD RISK

Larceny, according to the FBI, is "the unlawful taking or stealing of property or articles without the use of force, violence or fraud. It includes crimes such as shoplifting, pocket picking, purse snatching, thefts from motor vehicles, thefts of motor vehicle parts and accessories, bicycle thefts, etc." Shoplifting accounts for 8 to 10 percent of all larcenies. Larceny is the fastest growing crime category in the United States.

It was nearly 5:00 P.M. Pam, sixteen, and her best friend, Sandra, also sixteen, were doing some last-minute shopping at the supermarket for Pam's mother. They were only getting a few items—some milk, bread, a head of lettuce, and some lemon pie filling. Sandra stopped at the aisle filled with candy.

"Let's get some M&M's," she said.

"I don't think we have enough money," Pam replied. "Mom only gave me three dollars."

"Oh, we don't need money, let's just take them."

A look of mild surprise crossed Pam's face. Then she broke into a smile.

"Okay," she said, her eyes brightening. "You get the M&M's. I'm going to get some tuna fish. Mom say it's too expensive, but I love it."

Pam crossed the aisle and slid two cans of tuna fish into her jacket pocket, after looking up and down the deserted aisle several times, while Sandra opened her purse and dropped a family size bag of M&M's into it. Then they walked up to the checkout counter together, trying desperately to stifle an attack of giggles.

They paid for their other food items and went out the exit door. As they did, the store's assistant manager raced out after them.

"Girls," he said as he caught up with them, "would you please step back into the store for a minute. I'd like to talk to you."

The impulsive lark the girls had experienced only moments before suddenly turned into heart-stopping fear. Pam and Sandra exchanged a glance at each other. But just as quickly, the fear was replaced by indignation.

"Are you talking to us?" Sandra asked in a defiant tone. "We haven't done anything. What do you want with us?"

"Just step inside, please," the assistant manager said more firmly.

Sandra started to argue, but to avoid embarrassment, she and Pam went in with the manager and he took them through a door into the "Employees Only" section of the store, into a small office.

"I told you we didn't do anything," Sandra snapped. Pam's eyes dropped to a spot on the floor.

"Would you please empty your pockets," the manager

said to Pam. "And would you please open your purse," he said, looking straight at Sandra.

"But why?" Sandra asked more contritely now, her confidence shaken by the manager's persistence. There were a few seconds of silence, seconds that seemed to the girls like long minutes.

"We don't have to show you anything," Sandra finally managed to say. "You have no right."

"All right, girls," the manager said. "Have it your way." He picked up the phone and dialed a number.

"Sergeant Holmes," he said, "I have two juvenile shoplifters here at the market. We observed them concealing items in their jacket and purse and they left the store without paying for them. Now they refuse to admit they took anything. Could you come over and pick them up? Thanks."

"That's not very cool," Sandra said. "Okay, so we took a bag of candy and some tuna fish. Big deal. What does it cost, two dollars, three dollars? We'll pay you for it. Now can we go?"

"I'm sorry, girls," the manager said. "But shoplifting is stealing."

"But we're juveniles. We're under age. You can't do anything to us," Sandra said, still with arrogance.

A few minutes later a uniformed policeman entered the office, and the girls took out their stolen items and put them on the desk. The officer read them their rights, including the right to remain silent.

Pam and Sandra stared at each other in disbelief.

"Okay, girls, please come along with me," the officer said.

"But you're treating us just like criminals," Sandra

stammered. Pam started sobbing. "How can you arrest us just for shoplifting?" Sandra asked, as tears started to well up in her eyes too.

In the young men's section of the department store, Dave, seventeen, tried on an expensive leather jacket. It was priced at $169. It fit him perfectly. Dave looked around and saw that the only clerk on duty in the section was busy helping another teen try on a sports coat.

Dave grabbed the hanging price tag on the left sleeve of the jacket with his right hand and ripped it off with a quick jerk. He then strode through the store, wearing the jacket, and walked out the door. A second later, a uniformed guard, actually one of the city's policemen whom the store hired in their off-duty hours as security officers, ran out after Dave.

He caught up with him and asked him to come back into the store. Dave, panicking, started to run, but the officer caught him after a few strides. Then Dave tried to break free from the officer's grip on his arm. He struggled violently. The officer took Dave's left arm and pinned it behind his back in a painful position. Dave stopped resisting. The policeman then snapped a pair of handcuffs around Dave's wrists, clinging them together behind his back.

Dave couldn't believe what was happening. A crowd of shopping-mall onlookers was fast gathering, as the officer led Dave back toward the store.

"You can't do this to me," Dave pleaded. "I'm a minor. I'm under eighteen. You can't arrest me."

"Come on," the officer said, firmly clasping Dave by the arm as they walked briskly back to the department store.

Pam, Sandra, and Dave—all three representing ficticious names but true incidents—are representative of a disturbing phenomenon that is recurring thousands of times each week all across the United States and Canada. The plain fact is that most teen-agers do not realize how serious an offense shoplifting is. Many do not even know it's a crime. Most teens are totally ignorant of the laws governing larceny, which cover shoplifting, and of the penalties for breaking those laws. A great majority of young people believe that if they are caught, the worst that can happen to them is a lecture and they will have to pay for the goods they stole.

Today, merchants hear just about every excuse imaginable from apprehended shoplifters, such as:

—"But I just did it for kicks, for fun. There was no harm done."

—"You shouldn't punish me. I'll never do it again."

—"I was going to pay for it, I just forgot."

—"Why are you wasting your time holding me, when there are real criminals running loose?"

—"I was going to pay you the next time I came to the store."

—"So you caught me. So what. You can't do anything to me, I'm a juvenile."

Merchants, police officers, juvenile authorities, and judges have heard every answer imaginable. Yet ignorance of the law is no excuse and no defense against prosecution and conviction.

"We've found that many students had no idea of stores' losses as a result of shoplifting," says Jack Hayes, former security chief for Boston's Jordan Marsh department store. "They considered shoplifting a minor incident in which no one was hurt. The majority of them were also under the impression that if apprehended they would just be talked to and released."

"It's sad, but kids seem to think if they steal, the first time the police will take no action," adds a Toronto Youth Bureau officer. "They don't think they are committing a crime and are unaware what damage an arrest or conviction can have on their lives."

A nineteen-year-old girl in Madison, Wisconsin, recalls with horror the day she got caught shoplifting: "I thought they'd accept my apology, take the money and let me go. But I was wrong. The store owner, tired of theft, decided to press charges against me. By this time I was so scared I shook and my stomach felt like lead.

"When the police came," she says, "they didn't take me down to the station and book me. Instead, they read me my rights and told me to see the county district attorney in two days. I went home and cried all night. I was still scared, and there was no one to talk to. I didn't want my friends or parents to know.

"I spent the most degrading day of my life two days later. Before seeing the district attorney I went to the police station to be fingerprinted. They took about fifty prints: four cards each of each separate finger and one card with a full print of each hand. I kept thinking, 'This is it; I'm a criminal with a police record.' After the prints came the photos, or mug shots. A view from the front and one from the side. I could barely keep from bursting into tears."

In some states, the fingerprinting of teen-age shoplifters is becoming standard procedure. In Pennsylvania, for example, the law reads: "Prior to the commencement of trial or entry of plea of a defendant 16 years of age or older accused of the summary offense of retail theft, the issuing authority shall order the defendant to submit within five days of such order for fingerprinting by the municipal police of the jurisdiction in which the offense allegedly was committed, or the state police. Fingerprints so obtained shall be forwarded immediately to the Pennsylvania State Police . . ."

The days of light reprimands and lectures are declining. Regardless of their parents' financial or other status, teenagers caught shoplifting today are more than likely to wind up in juvenile court. Or, if they are eighteen or over in most states, and sixteen or over in some states, they will be called before an adult court and treated as adults.

"Youngsters rarely realize how a shoplifting arrest or conviction may damage their lives," says Delmar Dawkins, who has worked in the Juvenile Division of the Champaign, Illinois, Police Department. He points out that for such an offense, young people have later been denied security clearance for sensitive jobs, admission to certain colleges and professions, jobs requiring a bond or state license, civil service posts, and even, in extremes, they have been denied voting rights.

"Though technically, a juvenile's arrest record is expunged when he or she becomes an adult," Dawkins says, "most job applicants are asked the question, 'Were you ever arrested?' How do they answer that?"

In fact, many people have the mistaken idea that because special laws of confidentiality protect juveniles, their police records will remain secret forever. This isn't necessarily so, says Juvenile Court Judge William E. Gladstone of Dade County, Florida. "There is much less confidentiality about juvenile records than we would like to believe," he explains. "Agencies such as the Army, for example, will not take you unless you sign a form authorizing the court to give up its records. Colleges may ask such questions as 'Have you ever been arrested?' " And, Judge Gladstone says, although juvenile records are supposed to be destroyed after a period of time (usually five years after the incident), they sometimes wind up in computer banks and may stay in existence for years after they should have been destroyed.

Of course, with teen-agers who are of adult age, shoplifting arrest records last a lifetime.

Aside from the future repercussions a single shoplifting incident may cause, there often is an accompanying great amount of personal embarrassment. John W. Rhoads, chief of police in Prince Georges County, Maryland, says, "An arrest for shoplifting certainly will mean humiliation. There is a lasting stigma attached to being arrested."

This is becoming more and more prevalent across the nation as area newspapers, in cooperation with merchants, law-enforcement officials, and juvenile authorities are publishing names of teen-age offenders in states where there are no laws prohibiting such publication. Curtis Harris, former district attorney in Oklahoma City, Oklahoma, is one who believes such public exposure would help cut down on the teen-age thievery. "Shoplifting's allure would be tremendously dampened if juvenile-court secrecy (in some states) didn't bar public identification of youthful offenders," he says.

Recently, the Cleveland, Tennessee, *Daily Banner* began publishing names of juveniles charged with misdemeanors and felonies to determine whether the publicity would deter delinquency. "I've wrestled with this some because this has been taboo for as long as I've been in the news business," says Editor Beecher Hunter. "It's going against everything I've been taught, but I'm convinced there may be some merit to it."

There are thousands of case histories of damaged lives and careers resulting from what teen-agers thought were "harmless pranks of shoplifting." An eighteen-year-old honor graduate from an Eastern state, for example, was denied entrance to the United States Naval Academy, after recommendation by one of his congressmen, because a military security check revealed that he had once been convicted for stealing some soda pop.

A seventeen-year-old girl, a straight-A student in her California high school class, shoplifted a two-dollar costume jewelry brooch. She denied the theft to the police and so, automatically, had to appear before the juvenile court for a hearing. She was found guilty, and since her record as a juvenile could not be expunged until she was twenty-one, she was refused admission at the university she wanted to attend to study for a career as a lawyer.

A sixteen-year-old boy from New York, son of prominent parents, was arrested and convicted for stealing a tennis racquet from a sporting goods store. A few years after when he applied for a well-paying job with the federal government, a routine security check turned up the arrest record and he didn't get the job.

Leonard Kolodny of the Metropolitan Washington Board of Trade's Retail Bureau, says, "Young people are playing Russian roulette with their futures when they shoplift. Unfortunately, many of them don't realize it." And the National Retail Merchants Association reports that "harmless shoplifting sprees ruin the lives of far too many teens who didn't realize that stealing for kicks earned them permanent criminal records."

The NRMA says: "With a police record it can be difficult, in some cases impossible, to go into any business or profession where a special license is required, such as law, insurance, or real estate brokerage." It may be difficult, if not impossible, to obtain a passport. A criminal record also may prevent teens from obtaining a license as a doctor, lawyer, professional engineer, social worker, veterinarian, surveyor, optician, dentist, certified public accountant, nurse, architect, and many other similar occupations.

In its booklet, *Teenagers Beware: Shoplifting is Stealing*, the NRMA says many teens declare: "But I'm a juvenile. Nothing can happen to me!" The NRMA warns: "Don't you believe it! True, there are separate laws governing criminal acts by juveniles in most states, but an arrest is still an arrest, and a police record is still a police record. One shoplifting conviction can ruin your life.

"Many young people feel they can keep a juvenile record for a minor offense a secret," the booklet states. "Don't you believe it: Very often, juvenile police bureaus will answer an inquiry by reporting that a teenager has been declared a 'delinquent.' This description can include a serious crime.

"Although youngsters may go 'free' after an apprehension, once arrested, the charge will follow them demanding explanation and causing embarrassment whenever it reappears. Those 'kicks' can come back and haunt you forever. A minor record easily becomes a major problem."

JAIL!

Jail!

Detention homes. Prison. County farms. Work details. Training centers. The penitentiary.

Arrest and conviction for shoplifting, regardless of the amount taken, or whether it was the first offense or the tenth, can lead to serving time in jail and, also, substantial fines. This is true both for teen-agers who are treated as adults (eighteen or over in most states), and for juveniles under eighteen.

While the actual laws and penalties vary considerably from state to state and in Canada, there are some general points of consensus. In most states, for example, shoplifting crimes generally fall into two basic categories— misdemeanors and felonies. Felonies are much more serious crimes. The determining line distinguishing the two usually is fixed by the value of the goods stolen. In Virginia, for instance, if the value is $100 or more, the shoplifting is classified as a felony. In Ohio, the amount separating misdemeanor from felony is $150, and in West Virginia, it is $200. There are also two different types of

shoplifting, according to several state laws. One is concealment. That is where a person hides a stolen object in their
pocket, under their coat, in their purse, or in any other
place where it is not visible, and then attempts to leave the
store without paying for the object. The other form is usually called petty larceny, or petit larceny. This is where a
person carries out an item or items in full view, without
attempting to pay for them. If the item or items are of
sufficient value, anywhere from $100 up in most states,
this form of shoplifting is then called grand larceny, and
is a felony.

A better understanding of the precise nature of the
laws involving shoplifting can be obtained by studying a
specific state statute. Pennsylvania, for example, defines
shoplifting under its "Retail Theft Statute, Number
3929," as follows:

> A person is guilty of a retail theft if he (or she):
> (1) takes possession of, carries away, transfers or causes to be
> carried away or transferred, any merchandise displayed, held,
> stored, or offered for sale by any store or other retail mercantile
> establishment with the intention of depriving the merchant of
> the possession, use or benefit of such merchandise without pay-
> ing the full retail value thereof;
> (2) alters, transfers or removes any label, price tag marking,
> indicia of value or any other markings which aid in determining
> value affixed to any merchandise displayed, held, stored or
> offered for sale in a store or other retail mercantile establish-
> ment and attempts to purchase such merchandise personally
> or in consort with another at less than the full retail value with
> the intention of depriving the merchant of the full value of such
> merchandise;
> (3) transfers any merchandise displayed, held, stored or
> offered for sale by any store or other retail mercantile estab-
> lishment from the container in or on which the same shall be dis-

played to any other container with intent to deprive the merchant of all or some part of the full value thereof.

Many states have similar laws. The U.S. Department of Commerce, in its booklet, *The Cost of Crimes Against Business,* says: "Most state legislatures have enacted laws designed to combat shoplifting. A typical shoplifting law specifies the actions which are illegal under the terms of the act. These often include removing merchandise from the premises with intent to steal it, switching price tags, concealing merchandise with the intention of stealing it, and other actions. It is often not necessary that the merchandise be removed from the premises in order to establish guilt. The laws of most jurisdictions give the businessperson the right to detain suspected shoplifters within limits, without the danger of false arrest charges."

In many states, laws and penalties also apply to persons who help others shoplift. According to the Virginia Anti-Shoplifting Committee, for example: "Fines and imprisonments also apply to those convicted of willfully concealing merchandise, altering price tags, transferring goods from one container to another, or *assisting or aiding* another to do such things, with the intent to use goods without paying the full price."

The laws covering shoplifting have been tightened and updated in recent years to keep pace with the changing nature of the crime. Only a relatively short time ago, there were few statutes or laws dealing with price tag switching, for instance. Today, many states have amended their codes to take this more recent form of stealing into account.

What are the penalties for shoplifting, as prescribed by law? They vary greatly from state to state. And there is

a difference in the severity of penalties depending upon
the age of the offender. In most states, juveniles are
treated separately. They go through a juvenile court system, whereas young people eighteen and over (sixteen
and over in New York State) are handled through adult
criminal or district court systems.

The actual penalties can range from a reprimand and
release to sentences of several years in prison and fines
in the thousands of dollars. It all depends on whether the
shoplifter has a previous record; whether he or she has
been caught stealing before; the age of the shoplifter; the
value of the item or items taken; and, in some cases, on
the attitude of the thief after apprehension. A Virginia
judge recently fined a teen-age shoplifter and sentenced
him to time in jail for stealing a fifteen-cent candy bar.

Roger K. Griffin, head of Commercial Service Systems,
Inc., which keeps statistics on shoplifters for supermarkets
and drugstores in California, says: "Although laws and
sentencing for shoplifting differ throughout the country,
a $100 fine and jail time for shoplifters is a very common
occurrence."

California, in fact, has enacted a new law covering
shoplifting. It permits merchants to detain a suspected
shoplifter when they "reasonably believe" the person is
trying to steal merchandise. It also provides a mandatory
fine of from $50 to $1,000, for those eighteen and over,
for each such violation. And the law holds the parent or
guardian responsible for up to $500 if a minor is in-
volved."

Virginia law carries a maximum penalty of up to one
year in jail or up to $1,000 fine, or both, for shoplifting
goods valued at less than $100, and up to twenty years

in the penitentiary for shoplifting goods valued at $100 or more.

In Canada, the *Toronto Star* reports, "If the theft is worth more than $200, it could mean a maximum sentence of ten years." In Tennessee, shoplifters stealing merchandise valued under $100 face a fine of up to $300 and imprisonment for "not more than six months," or both. Thefts over $100 are charged as grand larceny and the penalties are much stiffer.

The West Virginia law says any convicted shoplifter "shall be confined in the county jail not less than one day nor more than twelve months, or fined not less than five dollars nor more than $500, or both fined and imprisoned." Thefts over $50 are classified as felonies, and those convicted "shall be confined in the penitentiary not less than one nor more than ten years, and fined not more than $1,000." Further, West Virginia law says, "an act of shoplifting is hereby declared to constitute a breach of the peace, and any citizen of the state may arrest a person committing any such act of shoplifting in his (or her) presence." No mention or distinction of adult or teen-age shoplifting is made under the present statute.

In Maine, thefts of merchandise under the value of $500 are categorized as "Class E" crimes. These are punishable by fines up to $500, and by imprisonment "not to exceed six months."

The New Hampshire Criminal Code states: "Larceny (including shoplifting) is punishable by five years imprisonment if the value of the property stolen exceeds $500, and by eleven months or $1,000 (fine) if it does not."

In Alaska, convicted shoplifters may be fined up to

$500 and imprisoned for not more than six months, or both. Under Ohio law, "shoplifted merchandise valued less than $150 is a first degree misdemeanor on the first offense and carries a maximum penalty of six months in jail and a fine not to exceed $1,000. The second conviction, regardless of the value of the property stolen, is a fourth degree felony with a sentence of two to five years and a maximum fine of $2,500."

In New York, according to Mary Lou McGanney of the Division of Criminal Justice Services, "Youngsters under sixteen years (and over seven years) are by definition 'juveniles.' They are not charged with shoplifting or petty larceny, but rather are charged with juvenile delinquency. All juvenile delinquency cases are heard in Family Court, and penalties are set at the discretion of the trial judge. These range from reprimands to stays of up to eighteen months in a training school."

Idaho has a relatively new shoplifting law under which those eighteen and over can receive a six-month jail sentence and a $300 fine for petty theft. The jail sentence increases to a maximum of fourteen years for thefts exceeding $150. Persistent juvenile shoplifters may end up in a rehabilitation center; however, penalties vary depending on the age and record of the offender.

In Kansas, judges have wide discretion in juvenile shoplifting cases, which are classified in complaints of delinquency (theft over $50), or miscreancy (theft under $50). The judge can, for example:

"(1) Place the youth on probation in the care, custody and control of either or both parents.

"(2) Place the youth in the care, custody and control of a duly appointed juvenile probation officer or other suitable person.

"(3) Place the youth in a detention home, parental home or farm.

"(4) Place the youth, if sixteen years old or over, in the county jail pending final disposition.

"(5) Commit the youth to the state secretary of social and rehabilitation services.

"(6) Commit the youth, if a boy thirteen years old or older, to the youth center at Topeka or other training or rehabilitation facility for juveniles; or, if a girl thirteen years old or older, to the youth center at Beloit or other training or rehabilitation facility for juveniles."

In Michigan, stealing from a store can be a felony, with a penalty of as much as four years' imprisonment, no matter how little is taken. And in Maryland, if the shoplifted goods retail for more than $100, a convicted thief can be jailed for up to three years.

Alabama has no separate shoplifting laws for juveniles and adults. All shoplifting laws fall into one of two categories: larceny and grand larceny. Anything shoplifted from within a store with a value less than $25 is larceny. Anything over $25 is grand larceny. The penalty for larceny, under shoplifting statutes, is a jail term of not more than one year at hard labor at a county work farm, as well as a possible $500 fine, should the judge decree. Grand larceny calls for a prison term of not less than one year and not more than ten years.

The state of Utah is proving that one effective means of reducing teen-age theft is through more direct involvement with parents and with parents' pocketbooks. In 1975, the Utah state legislature passed a new law that provides for parents being held responsible for the costs— up to $1,000—incurred by children for shoplifting.

The Utah Criminal Justice Administration reports this

law, along with a concerted statewide and state-funded anti-shoplifting educational campaign, has resulted in a 25 percent reduction in the amount and value of merchandise stolen, and a corresponding increase, of 10 percent, in the percentage of teen-age shoplifting convictions.

COMING TO COURT

You are a teen-ager under the age of eighteen and you have just been caught shoplifting. What happens next? Will you have to go to court and appear before a judge? Will you be fined? Will you go to jail or to a juvenile detention home? What, realistically, can you expect?

Again, the procedure may vary somewhat from state to state, but the following sequence of events, based on in-depth interviews with juvenile authorities, state prosecuting attorneys and juvenile judges, would be likely to occur.

First, the merchant involved makes a complaint, or decides to press charges. Many stores make this a mandatory policy today. The merchant may call in the police. Either the merchant or the police then will take the teen-ager to an intake officer. This is a person who works for a city or a county juvenile service. They may be called different things in different states—social worker, juvenile authority, probation officer, or something else.

The intake officer is the contact person between the community and the court. Let's suppose, in this case, that the officer is a woman and the teen-ager is a boy. She sits down with the teen-ager, the complaining merchant, and usually the police officer who has been called in. She then takes down the facts of the case. The merchant tells how the thief was caught stealing in the store and what was stolen.

If the teen-ager wants to say something at this time, he can, but it's almost always pointless to deny the shoplifting because the merchant would not take such drastic action unless he was sure.

The intake officer, after getting the full story of the theft, then sets an appointment for the boy and his parents. This is usually within a few days. At this meeting, if it is the first time the teen-ager has ever been caught stealing and has never been arrested before, and he readily admits that he is guilty of the shoplifting charge and is repentant about it, the officer will take all this into consideration. She also will be interested in the parents' attitude. Are they shocked, or are they complacent and non-caring? The officer likely will ask the parents if they travel much in their jobs, and how much time they spend at home. She will ask the parents if their son is a discipline problem, or causes any trouble at home.

If it is a first offense and the boy is sincerely sorry about it and has learned the lesson never to steal again, and the officer senses this, as opposed to phony sob stories which she hears every day, then the case may be settled without having to go to court. If the officer sees that the teen-ager has responsible and caring parents, she may release him to be placed under their cognizance. That is, instead of putting him on any formal probation, she will, in effect, ask his parents to be responsible, and serve as unofficial parole officers at home.

She will also see that the boy repays the merchant for the value of the items stolen, and, usually, that he be barred from shopping at that store, or others like it if it is a chain store, for a period of a year or more.

If, however, the intake officer feels that the "experience of appearing in court" would be remedial, or beneficially instructive, she will recommend that. This is more likely the case if the teen-ager has been caught shoplifting before, or had a prior arrest record, or if he had been in previous trouble with juvenile authorities. The officer also is more likely to recommend sending the teen-ager through the court process if he does not openly admit being guilty of shoplifting, despite substantial evidence to the contrary, or if a defiant or authority-challenging attitude is shown. ("You can't do anything to me, I'm a juvenile.") The officer probably will recommend court appearance if the parents are not fully cooperative. ("We know our rights. We'll get a lawyer. Who is your boss, anyway? We want to speak to him.")

So, for these or other reasons, the boy may be ordered to appear in court before a judge. In fact, in some areas, juvenile court judges demand that all shoplifters appear before them, whether it's a first offense or not, and regardless of the circumstances. These judges feel that an appearance before them, by a teen-ager in the sobering environment of the courtroom, helps act as a strong deterrent against repeating criminal offenses.

A court date is set, again usually within a few days of the first meeting with the intake officer. The boy and his parents are told to appear at a certain date. They may have to wait several hours before seeing the judge, depending on how busy that day's docket is.

At this initial hearing, the charges are explained by

the judge and the boy is informed of his right to remain silent if he wishes. If his parents have not retained an attorney, the judge may appoint one. If the family cannot afford an attorney, one will be provided without cost. The judge then sets a trial date. If the boy comes from a broken home—say, for example, if his father no longer lives at home and his mother is an alcoholic—the judge may assign the boy to a foster home, or to a detention center until the trial date comes up. But this is rare.

The next stage is the trial. With juvenile cases, there are no juries—only the judge. This trial is often called an "adjudicatory hearing." It is similar to adult trials in some respects. The issue of guilt or innocence will be decided. Testimony is taken, witnesses are called to the stand, and in giving their evidence, they may be cross-examined by the defense lawyer or by the prosecuting attorney.

As the defendant, the boy does not have to testify. After hearing all the evidence, the judge alone decides whether the boy is guilty or not guilty of shoplifting. Once a juvenile case reaches the court, rarely is the defendant found not guilty.

The boy is found guilty by the judge and is classified as an adjudicated delinquent (this term may vary from state to state). But the case is not over yet. The judge then sets a date for a third court appearance—at which the boy will be sentenced. This is generally called a "dispositional hearing." Usually, this may be anywhere from a few days to several weeks after the trial. This time is needed for the intake officer or social worker to draft a detailed paper called, in many states, a "pre-disposition report."

This is, in effect, a complete "social history" of the teen-ager and his family. The judge will use this as background material to help reach a fair sentence. The intake officer, through interviews with the boy and his family and by other research, will cover such subject matter as: any previous arrest record or trouble he may have gotten into; the environment of his home; school work; what the mother and father do, and what kind of influence they have on their son; who the boy's friends are and what effect their relationship has on his behavior; and other topics.

This report usually runs several typewritten pages. When the intake officer completes it, she then makes a recommendation to the judge, based on the findings made during the research for the report. These recommendations can range anywhere from unsupervised probation to detention in a juvenile home or training center. The judge does not have to follow the recommendation of the intake officer, but often considers it very important in rendering a decision. This is especially true in crowded courts in cities and large urban areas where the judges are overburdened with heavy case loads.

The boy then reports for the third court appearance, or dispositional hearing. Most judges like to keep this session as informal and relaxed as possible. This is the time when the judge, the boy and his parents, and the intake officer work together to agree on a program best suited to the teen-ager's specific case.

Here, the judge has to consider the boy's needs, the needs of his parents for assistance, protection of the community, and other factors. The basic aim is to find the best solution for the problem. The judge is limited somewhat by state statutes in what can be done. However, in most areas, juvenile court judges have considerable leeway in the amount and degree of punishment they order.

If the boy is lucky, he may receive a warning and admonition from the judge, who may decree that he can return home to his parents and be put on what is called unsupervised probation. The judge then is placing prime responsibility for future behavior on the boy and his parents. The judge will often bar the boy from reentering the store where he shoplifted.

The judge may add some conditions to this type of probation, such as ruling that the boy not miss any school classes unless he is ill. Many judges in many areas of the United States and Canada order juvenile shoplifters to a certain period of "volunteer" community service work. Such programs have become very popular in recent years. The boy may be assigned to work in the community library, or cut grass, wash windows, and rake leaves. Or he may wash police cars and fire engines. Judges consider this good, because it gets offenders outdoors, and they feel it is therapeutic.

Or, the boy may be placed on supervised probation, and assigned to a juvenile authority or probation officer. The boy must sign a formal set of rules agreed to by him, the judge, the parents and juvenile officials. Under these terms, the teenager must report in to his assigned officer periodically. A nightly curfew may be set, and a responsible adult may have to know where the boy is at all times. The period of this supervised probation varies, but from six months to a year is common.

Some juvenile judges have found that suspension of a teen-ager's driver's license proves to be a highly effective deterrent. In some states, judges may suspend a driver's license for non-highway crimes, such as shoplifting.

Depending on the circumstances, the boy can be fined.

In most states, the maximum fine can be as much as five hundred dollars. If the judge decides his family life at home is not conducive to proper rehabilitation, that is, if the judge feels the boy will not receive adequate supervision and guidance at home, he may be ordered to move in with other relatives, or to move into a foster home. Or the judge may sentence the boy to a juvenile home or training or learning center.

If the boy is sixteen or over in many states, or fifteen or over in some, and the judge determines that he is "not amenable to treatment," or if he has committed a felony, he can be transferred to adult court and sentenced to jail. This most often happens to shoplifters who have been arrested repeatedly and have not learned their lesson under previous sentencing. In many areas, the boy could be sentenced up to a year in jail.

Of course, if he is eighteen or over (sixteen or over in New York), he will go through the adult court system. No intake officer is involved here, and the penalties and sentences generally are much stronger. He can be sentenced to a heavy fine and a jail term even for a first offense. Many judges make it mandatory to serve at least one day in jail, believing this to be an effective deterrent to crime, especially with young people. A common sentence for a first-time shoplifter who is eighteen or over may be a fine of fifty to one hundred dollars and a jail sentence of fifteen to thirty days with all but one day suspended.

Fines and jail terms usually go up sharply for shoplifters who have been arrested before.

Many judges, juvenile authorities, and others believe the fact that teen-agers must appear in court acts as a deterrent in itself against the commission of further crimes. It has a strong effect, both on juveniles and on their parents.

"I don't see many repeat shoplifter offenders, particularly from middle- or upper-class families," says Juvenile Court Judge Herbert Field of Gloucester, Virginia. "When parents receive a summons to appear in court with their child they generally are shocked. And almost every kid I see in court is scared. They may laugh and say they don't mind going, but that's not true. The court process has impact. A juvenile may laugh and joke about it with his or her peers after they get out of court, but I think that's just a release mechanism. They are scared in court, and this is where the court can be an effective deterrent. We treat it as very serious business, and the message gets across.

"The whole juvenile program is geared to rehabilitation," explains Judge Field. "We do not consider shoplifting a minor crime. We intend to turn the young offenders around before they become adult criminals."

SOME ANSWERS
TO THE PROBLEM

What are the best long-term solutions to the teen-age shoplifting problem? What programs and actions would be most effective in curbing or detecting this widespread crime, the consequences of which can so seriously mar the futures of young people who succumb to its temptations?

We have examined some steps that have been taken by concerned merchants and communities. Certainly, stepped-up security and the use of advanced electronic systems and other safeguards in stores provide some protection. And they result in the apprehension and arrest of more shoplifters.

The community-wide educational programs, such as the ones annually promoted in Philadelphia, Washington, Champaign, Illinois, and in other cities and areas in the United States and Canada, also have proved to have a positive deterrent effect in cutting down on the occurrence rates of shoplifting. This is done by making teen-agers aware of the seriousness of the crime, pointing out how it hurts everyone, and by demonstrating how the penalties for being caught can be severely damaging to young people.

But for lasting solutions to the shoplifting problem, more has to be done. One area where improvement is needed is in the courts. While state anti-shoplifting laws have been strengthened and penalties have been stiffened in recent years in most areas, the laws have not been uniformly enforced and carried through the judicial system.

The principal reason for this is that the courts, the police, and juvenile officers and personnel assigned to supervise sentenced teen-age shoplifters, are often overcrowded and overworked.

A magazine reporter doing an article on shoplifting, for example, was at a store in a busy shopping center in the San Fernando Valley near Los Angeles when a teen-age shoplifter was apprehended and held. The police were immediately called, but no one arrived for more than two hours. Finally an officer showed up. He apologized for the delay, explaining that he had made twenty-six other arrests that afternoon in that shopping center alone. With more and more merchants enforcing "get-tough" policies with shoplifters—in many cases following mandatory arrest policies—courts and juvenile offices, already jammed up, are becoming inundated.

One store manager in New York City reports he waited fourteen and a half hours in court to testify in the prosecution of one shoplifter. He said it would have been cheaper and less trouble to drop charges. And even when merchants wait it out for hours, sometimes days, to bring charges, they often find that judges mete out light sentences amounting to little more than a slap on the wrist of the shoplifter, to get the case disposed of as quickly as possible.

Says Robert Sakowitz, President of Sakowitz, Houston, a chain of specialty stores in Texas: "The courts are not helping. They're overburdened and frequently found to be quite lenient." And, adds Leonard Kolodny of the Washington, D.C. Board of Trade's Retail Bureau: "Too many juvenile authorities, prosecutors, and judges still consider shoplifting a minor crime, so the net result is that shoplifting often is treated too lightly. The courts are overcrowded and juvenile offices are overcrowded. Uniformly harsher penalties would be one effective answer to the whole problem, but the judicial system does not have time or manpower to put these offenders through the system."

"When law enforcement is ineffective, much of the blame lies not with the police, but with the courts," says Alessandro Baccari, president of the San Francisco Council of District Merchants Associations. "Law for the policeman is a revolving door. He doesn't know what his duties are. We're going to have to make the judicial system aware of our concerns. When the courts start passing tougher sentences, that's when we'll get rid of criminals."

Still, there are ways even the busiest of prosecutors and judges can speed up the system and make it a more effective deterrent. A number of courts, realizing the problem, have instituted a system whereby retailers are called shortly before a case where they are to testify is coming up.

In New Orleans, one judge hears all shoplifting cases within two days of apprehension of the shoplifter, and he quickly penalizes those who don't want a trial. This system has been highly praised by merchants. But perhaps the best example of how to handle the crowded court problem has been set in Chicago. The Department of Commerce, in its booklet, *Crimes in Retailing,* reports: "To speed the processing of trials, the city of Chicago has established a special shoplifter's court. This step makes prosecution of shoplifting cases less time-consuming and reduces the expense for the victimized merchant."

Another key problem that must be overcome in the fight to reduce shoplifting can be classified as "customer apathy." Have you ever seen anyone shoplift in a store? Did you do anything about it? Unfortunately, most people who observe others stealing, even though they know it is wrong and that in the end it will cost them more through increased prices, do nothing.

Yet, if you and other shoppers report such crimes, if you see them, they can be a very effective deterrent to shoplifting. A professional shoplifter, cooperating with authorities after his arrest, had this to say: "A store's customers can be impressive shoplifting preventatives. If a person sees someone stealing and reports the incident to a salesperson or a security guard, the crime can be stopped. But most people don't want to get involved, or they simply don't care."

In a research study on "Consumer Attitudes Toward Shoplifting," Dr. Leonard W. Prestwich, professor of marketing at the University of Nebraska at Omaha, found the following: "Those [shoppers who observed someone shoplifting] and said they would do nothing were asked why. Their main reasons, in order of importance, were: 'None of my business'; 'Don't want to get involved'; 'It is futile to take action'; 'Sympathy for the shoplifter'; 'Items of small value do not warrant action'; 'Too busy'; 'Afraid of legal action'; 'Afraid of physical harm'; and 'I shoplift.'"

In fact, more than 21 percent of those surveyed, or

about one of every five persons, gave answers that reflected either a neutral or a proshoplifting attitude. Nearly all of these respondents said they would do nothing if they saw someone else stealing.

In his study conclusions, Dr. Prestwich said: "There are significant numbers of consumers who do not recognize that shoplifting increases prices for consumers, who see little reason to be concerned about the problem, and who exhibit neutral and proshoplifting attitudes. These consumers are primarily in the younger age groups."

Juvenile authorities agree that by reporting shoplifters, you are doing a service that not only may lower the cost of products for you and others, but also, more importantly, you may be helping the person you report stealing. Otherwise, if not caught, that person may go on stealing and graduate to more serious crimes. Therefore, reporting store theft is in the best interests of everyone—you, the merchant, the community, and the shoplifter.

Juvenile authorities, sociologists, psychologists, and other experts say that perhaps the most effective key of all to curbing the teen-age shoplifting problem lies in the home. No matter what police, educators, or other interested agencies do in the struggle to stop theft by juveniles, the primary influence remains with parents. Many experts contend that all too many parents today are too permissive, overprotective of their children, refuse to believe their kids can do anything wrong, shrug responsibility for wrongful acts committed by their sons and daughters, or are apathetic and just don't care.

Some examples:

☐ In Brookfield, Connecticut, the parents of a fifteen-year-old were called by a merchant who apprehended their daughter after she stole $43 worth of merchandise.

The girl's father was a lawyer. The mother charged into the merchant's office and told her daughter, "Don't worry. I don't know what you did, but Daddy will get you out of it."

☐ In neighboring New Fairfield, Connecticut, a fourteen-year-old boy was caught stealing pens from a drugstore. When his mother arrived, she told the boy, "I want you to apologize." When he did, she exclaimed, "Today you are a man. I'm so proud of you I'm going to buy you a soda."

Noting that there was no hint of punishment or even disapproval, Connecticut probation officer Bernard Lynch says, "Such mothers are contributing to the delinquency of their own minors. This boy is bound to steal again. He thinks all he has to do is apologize when he gets caught."

☐ In Denver, a fourteen-year-old girl was arrested for shoplifting a dress. It turned out she had a whole closetful of stolen clothes at home. Her parents weren't even aware of it. Likewise, a boy in a northern New Jersey suburb was found to have twelve stolen $20 shirts in his closet. His parents said they had never noticed them.

☐ In Birmingham, Alabama, the parents of a sixteen-year-old boy, arrested for shoplifting several record albums, hired the best lawyer they could find because they refused to believe their son guilty, even though the evidence against him was overwhelming.

Many parents, experts say, don't want to face what are obvious truths. They prefer to turn their backs and ignore the facts in the futile hope that the problem will go away. It won't. It will only get worse.

Parents who would be horrified if told their children are thieves actually contribute to the problem through apathy and an unwillingness to discipline. Many teens openly display stolen items in their rooms and are never questioned about them. Even when parents suspect theft, they frequently are reluctant to act. This is especially true among middle- and upper-class families.

Dr. Ben J. Sheppard, former judge of Miami, Florida's Juvenile and Domestic Relations Court, says: "When anything expensive shows up in a lower-class home, the mother or father know it's stolen and usually act immediately. But upper middle-class parents are truly incredible. Their child may have a whole closet full of new clothes, and yet they'll buy the story that he or she traded with other kids. They never even bother to ask where that unexplained stereo set came from." Store security officers stress that parents finding questionable goods in their children's rooms should not accept flimsy explanations of where they came from. To do so, say the experts, will probably encourage further thievery.

"Since stealing is a crime rather than merely a family problem, all too many parents refuse to seek help even when they know their child is a thief," says Mrs. Jessie Johnson, head of the Family and Children's Service of Colorado. "By trying to cover up the situation, parents keep their children from getting the preventive assistance they need so badly," she adds. "And once the child has been arrested, it's too late to regret what should have been done long ago."

"Many parents are shocked when their children are caught stealing," says a Connecticut juvenile court judge. "They just can't imagine it. To them, shoplifting always happens somewhere else, to someone else. Yet, even when they learn about their children, many parents take a 'so what' attitude, as if it's no big deal," says the judge.

Speaking to this point, Drs. Michael Geurts and

Everett Johnston of the College of Business Administration, University of Hawaii, in their study, "Shoplifting: Deviant Consumer Behavior," concluded: "As long as delinquent behavior is considered 'normal' and socially acceptable, and as long as family and social sanctions are ineffective against peer-group support for unlawful conduct, the retailer and the public will continue to suffer the ill effects of shoplifting crime."

Thus, shoplifting, like other forms of crime, thrives to the extent that it is tolerated. And such toleration begins in the teen-ager's home.

Leo E. Wilson, mayor of Laurel, Maryland, in an open letter to his community's parents, says, "The most effective anti-shoplifting education begins at home." And John W. Rhoads, police chief of Prince Georges County, Maryland, adds, "Children should be taught that it is better to withstand peer-group pressures than to commit a crime." He says parents should realize shoplifting is a stepping-stone to more serious crime. "It must be curbed before a pattern of criminality is established," the chief warns.

What can be done? The National Retail Merchants Association, lists some suggestions:

☐ Be aware that shoplifting can be just the beginning of bigger trouble.

☐ Make sure you understand that shoplifting is stealing and stealing is a criminal act.

☐ Be certain that you know what a police record can do to chances for jobs, colleges, and professions.

☐ Find out what the community is doing about the shoplifting problem, and lend help.

☐ Understand that it is more "chicken" to go along with the crowd than to refuse to do so.

Of course, the ultimate answer to the billion-dollar-a-year shoplifting problem lies with the teen-ager. Is the permanent future of a young life worth the risk of a spur-of-the-moment temptation for taking an item that either isn't needed or is affordable?

Think about it.

BIBLIOGRAPHY

PERIODICALS AND PAMPHLETS

"Anti-Shoplifting Battle Heats Up." *U.S. News and World Report,* 28 November 1977.

"Antonia the Shoplifter." *Toronto Star,* 18 February 1974.

"Campaign to Convince Youngsters Shoplifting is a Crime Launched." *Security Management Magazine,* September 1974.

"Fighting the Costly War Against Stock Shortages." *Men's Wear Magazine,* 6 January 1978.

International Lutheran Laymen's League. (n.d.) *Danger—Hands Off.* St. Louis, Mo.

"Is There a Shoplifter in Your Family?" *Harper's Bazaar,* October 1971.

Men's Wear Retailers of America. (n.d.) *Everything Has a Price.* Washington, D.C.

Metropolitan Washington Board of Trade, Retail Bureau. (n.d.) *Shoplifting: A Game for Losers* (press kit). Washington, D.C. (Copyright.)

National Retail Merchants Association. (n.d.) *Teenagers Beware! Shoplifting is Stealing.* New York, N.Y.

"Philadelphia's Way of Stopping the Shoplifter." *Business Week,* 6 May 1972.

Prestwich, Leonard, Professor of Marketing, University of Nebraska at Omaha. "Consumer Attitudes Toward Shoplifting." Paper presented at a National Retail Merchants Association Conference, 10 January 1977.

"Shoplifting Among Students." *Journal of Retailing*, Fall 1974.

"Shoplifting: Deviant Consumer Behavior." *Retail Control Magazine*, March 1973.

"Shoplifting: It's Getting Out of Hand." *The Virginia Gazette*, 18 November 1977.

"Shoplifting—The $4 Billion Boost." *The Journal of Insurance*, January–February 1978.

"They Steal for the Hell of It." *Saturday Evening Post*, October 1968.

U.S. Department of Commerce, Bureau of Domestic Commerce, *The Cost of Crimes Against Business*. (n.d.)

————*Crime in Retailing*. (n.d.)

————*Federal Government Sources on Crimes Against Business*. (n.d.)

U.S. Department of Justice, Federal Bureau of Investigation, *Crime in the United States*, 1976.

U.S. Small Business Administration, *Preventing Retail Theft*. (n.d.)

————*Reducing Shoplifting Losses*. (n.d.)

Virginia Anti-Shoplifting Campaign (n.d.) *Shoplifting Ruins You*. Richmond, Va.

Virginia Commission for Children and Youth. (n.d.) *You Have the Right to Know It* (a Rights Responsibilities Handbook for Virginia Teenagers). Richmond, Va.

"Why Kids Steal." *Today's Health*, December 1970.

"Youthful Shoplifting: A National Epidemic." *Reader's Digest*, April 1967.

BOOKS

Cavan, Ruth S. *Juvenile Delinquency*, 3rd edition, Philadelphia: J. P. Lippincott, 1975.

Offer, Daniel. *Psychological World of the Teenager*, New York: Basic Books, 1973.

LIST OF ORGANIZATIONS TO WRITE TO
FOR FURTHER INFORMATION ON SHOPLIFTING

Federal Bureau of Investigation, U.S. Department of Justice, Washington, D.C., 20535.

Insurance Information Institute, 110 William Street, New York, N.Y., 10038.

Men's Wear Retailers of America, 390 National Press Building, Washington, D.C., 20045.

National Retail Merchants Association, 100 W. 31st Street, New York, N.Y., 10001.

Retail Bureau, Metropolitan Board of Trade, 1129 20th Street, NW, Washington, D.C., 20036.

U.S. Chamber of Commerce, 1615 H Street, NW, Washington, D.C.

U.S. Department of Commerce, Consumer Goods and Services Division, Washington, D.C., 20230.

U.S. Small Business Administration, 1441 L Street, NW, Washington, D.C.

INDEX